Britain's Railways in the
First World War

Also by Michael Foley

Britain's Railways in the Second World War
(Pen and Sword, 2020)

Britain's Railway Disasters:
Fatal Accidents from the 1830s to the Present Day
(Pen and Sword, 2019 & 2013)

The British Army of the Rhine
After the First World War
(Fonthill, 2017)

Prisoners of the British:
Internees and POWs during the First World War
(Fonthill, 2015)

Rise of the Tank:
Armoured Vehicles and their use in the First World War
(Pen and Sword, 2014)

Pioneers of Aerial Combat:
Air Battles of the First World War
(Pen and Sword, 2013)

Essex in the First World War
(History Press, 2009)

Hard as Nails:
The Sportsmen's Battalion of World War One
(Spellmount, 2007)

Essex: Ready for Anything
(Sutton Publishing, 2006)

Britain's Railways in the First World War

Michael Foley

PEN & SWORD
TRANSPORT

First published in Great Britain in 2021 by
Pen & Sword Transport
An imprint of
Pen & Sword Books Ltd
Yorkshire – Philadelphia

Copyright © Michael Foley 2021

ISBN 978 1 52678 679 1

A CIP catalogue record for this book is
available from the British Library.

Typeset by Mac Style
Printed and bound in Great Britain by
CPI Group (UK) Ltd, Croydon, CR0 4YY

Pen & Sword Books Limited incorporates the imprints of Atlas,
Archaeology, Aviation, Discovery, Family History, Fiction, History,
Maritime, Military, Military Classics, Politics, Select, Transport,
True Crime, Air World, Frontline Publishing, Leo Cooper, Remember
When, Seaforth Publishing, The Praetorian Press, Wharncliffe
Local History, Wharncliffe Transport, Wharncliffe True Crime
and White Owl.

For a complete list of Pen & Sword titles please contact

PEN & SWORD BOOKS LIMITED
47 Church Street, Barnsley, South Yorkshire, S70 2AS, England
E-mail: enquiries@pen-and-sword.co.uk
Website: www.pen-and-sword.co.uk

Or

PEN AND SWORD BOOKS
1950 Lawrence Rd, Havertown, PA 19083, USA
E-mail: Uspen-and-sword@casematepublishers.com
Website: www.penandswordbooks.com

To Liam and Lewis Oliver –
two little boys who changed my life for the better.

Contents

List of Illustrations

Note on illustrations

Unless otherwise acknowledged, the pictures in this book are from the author's own collection of postcards, magazines and old photograph albums and it has been impossible to determine if any copyright is attached to them. Any infringement of copyright as a result of their publication is entirely unintentional; if any copyright has been infringed, the author extends his apologies to the parties concerned. Should this have happened, please contact the author through the publisher.

Introduction

The view that war was coming was prevalent in the years leading up to 1914 and a number of preparations were already under way. It was because of this that the Railway Executive Committee was formed as early as 1912, its objective being to act as an intermediary between the government and the numerous British railway companies that existed at that time. When war was declared, the government took over 130 separately owned railway companies. This still left more than forty-six others that remained independent. These were either short or light railway systems.

In 1914 Britain had 23,000 miles of railway track and 4,000 stations. Between them, the many different railway companies were one of the country's largest employers, with more than 700,000 workers. At this time there was little competition in transport as the road system was not well developed and motor vehicles were still uncommon. Much of the road transport in rural areas was still drawn by horses. When the railway companies were taken over the Railway Executive Committee consisted of twelve members and staff.

By 4 August 1914 – the day that Britain declared war on Germany – the country's railway system had already become accustomed to moving large numbers of troops. This experience had been gained through transporting thousands of men back and forth to Territorial Army summer camps, where they would undertake two weeks' training. The camp sites were normally in remote areas, only accessible by train.

On the outbreak of war, the scale of troop transport that was needed increased dramatically as the railways had to move around 120,000 men as well as equipment across the country to Southampton on their way to France. The first troop train left Waterloo station on 10 August. Over the following weeks, a train full of troops reached the docks every twelve minutes for up to fourteen hours a day.

The number of troops that Britain could put into the field was low compared with our allies and the enemy. The nineteenth century had not seen a vast expansion of the British Army despite the size of the empire. Most of Britain's forces were overseas and there had been no home defence system until conflict with France threatened in the mid-nineteenth century and volunteer rifle units began to be formed. By 1860, these home defence volunteers numbered 120,000 men. These were the origins of the Territorial Army.

It was the Crimean War that was to show how important the railways were to the military. The terrible conditions that British troops endured were due to the problems of moving supplies to the front. It was this era that saw the connection between private railway employees and the military. Samuel Morton Peto, who had been instrumental in building the Great Western Railway, built a railway from Sebastopol to Balaklava.

It became obvious that the army did not just consist of fighting men; it needed an organised level of services to supply and support them. In 1856, a new corps called the Military Train was created. This was to become a permanent department of the army and its function was to convey stores, ammunition and equipment.

Apart from the Military Train, a volunteer railway branch was also formed in 1860. They were the first corps of engineers, a voluntary railway force. They were called the 1st Middlesex, South Kensington Engineers Volunteers. Then came the formation of the Engineer and Voluntary Staff Corps in 1865, which consisted only of officers, usually with railway experience.

The late nineteenth century saw a great increase in volunteer military units and this included another railway unit – the 2nd Cheshire Royal Engineers Railway Volunteers, which was formed in 1887 in Crewe. It consisted of 600 employees of the London and North Western Railway (L&NWR). They saw service in the Boer War and became part of the early railway force of the Royal Engineers.

The main objectives of the early railway units were to prepare the route, lay and maintain the permanent way and construct bridges and platforms. They were also to defend stations, make field works and, in extreme circumstances, destroy railways if there was a danger to their base and enemy troops were likely to use the railway. The Belgians destroyed

Figure 1 The 2nd Cheshire Railway Royal Engineers consisted of 600 employees of the L&NWR and were formed in Crewe in 1887.

their own lines and bridges to stop the Germans using them. Railway troops were to be involved in the Sudan and in the Boer Wars.

In 1896, the Army Railway Council was formed, which included six railway managers of four English railway companies, one Scottish company and one Irish company. They were brought together to organise the movement of troops in time of war. In 1911 the country was divided into six areas of command. Each had its own main railway company. The Eastern Command had the South East and Chatham Railway, London Command had the London and South Western Railway, Southern Command had the London and North Western Railway, Western Command had the North Eastern Railway, Scottish Command had the North British Railway, and Ireland Command had the Great Northern Railway of Ireland. These were known as the secretary companies.

The British Army had wide experience of military use of railways overseas in China and South Africa but unlike the other countries of Europe who could use their railways to invade neighbouring countries, being an island nation, Britain couldn't do so, so its military railways were not as fully developed.

Figure 1a An early military train carrying artillery and their 40-pounder guns.

The nations that were to become the main antagonists of the First World War were beginning to develop their railway systems with war in mind. The German Schlieffen Plan originated at the turn of the century but was taken over by Helmuth von Moltke in 1906 and was based on the belief that Russia, with its poor railway network, would not be able to mobilise its army quickly. Using their railway system, Germany could hope to overwhelm France before moving on to fight a still unprepared Russia.

The French had not been idle, however, and in the years leading up to the war they had been building numerous lines towards the German border. They also planned to mobilise their army using the railway system. In 1914, the French Chief of General Staff was Joseph Joffre, a former military engineer and railway expert. The French Plan XVII was the equivalent of the German plan.

The French were also dependent on their ally Russia, which needed to develop its own railway to meet the German threat. The German plan therefore had a disadvantage as the French helped finance improved Russian railway lines that would enable them to mobilise quickly.

Figure 2 The German Army had developed the country's railway system to aid their military plans to move their men into position before their enemies could prepare to meet them.

There was little need for Britain to build new lines in the event of war as they already had one of the best, if not *the* best, railway system in the world. What they did do was to draw up timetables to enable their forces to get to the Continent in time to help their allies. The managers of Britain's largest railway companies were already part of what was the secret Railway Executive Committee from 1912, and previous to that, a railway manual for war had been published by the government in 1911.

The improvements in the railway systems of each of the eventual antagonists could not be kept secret. The extension of railways was then in many ways part of the build-up to war as each country understood why the systems of others were being improved. They all knew that if one country began to mobilise then the others had to follow in case they were left behind.

In the years before the war the arms race was evident and was hardly kept secret. Harold Rudgard worked for the Midland Railway as a District Motive Power Superintendent. Rudgard was also a volunteer in the Territorial Army. In 1911 he was sent to Germany to study mass production of railway equipment at the Krupp's Railway Works. The production of railway material for military use and the building of armaments were evident and were reported back to Rudgard's military superiors on his return.

A fair number of the British troops who travelled to France would have been railway employees. The rail companies lost more than 100,000 of their workers through enlistment in the forces, many of whom were reservists. There were already around 13,000 women working on Britain's railways in 1914 but they were mainly involved in what were regarded as women's jobs such as cleaning and waitressing. There had been women working in other employment on the railways for some time before the war began; many level crossing gatekeepers, for instance, had been women. It was a job that fitted in with women's traditional family responsibilities and sometimes came with a rent-free home. There were also women with more technical skills who were employed in railway workshops. These were sewing machinists or wood polishers for the finishing of interiors of coaches. As the war progressed, women were increasingly taking on the roles conventionally filled by male railway workers who had joined the forces.

It is no surprise that so many of the staff joined the armed forces. At the time, many of the working-class population were very unfit and could not pass the medical for service; this was especially true of men from the large cities where there was widespread poverty. Men from the countryside tended to be fitter. This was claimed to be the case by American journalist and social activist Jack London in his 1903 book *The People of the Abyss*, after he spent time living with working-class people in London at the turn of the century. Things may have improved by the time the war began but his views would still have been relevant to a certain extent. He claimed that railway employees were among the elite of workers. There is no doubt that companies such as the Great Western Railway had a very modern healthcare system for their employees and their families at this time and it was this that was said to have been the model for the National Health Service when it was set up after the Second World War.

This would seem to be the case when one examines railway company literature from the pre-war period. Although education for the working class had become more widespread before the war and literacy rates for recruits to the forces was said to be over 60 per cent, how much interest in literature there was amongst the working class is debatable.

The *Great Eastern Railway Magazine* for 1914, however, gives the impression that company employees had high levels of literacy. The magazine had sections on music and art, and in each issue there were short stories, a women's page and a list of new books that had been added to the staff library at Liverpool Street Station.

Demand for railway services had grown even before the war began and in response to this, staff members of the Great Eastern Railway were expected to perform at a high level. Locomotives were becoming larger, heavier and more powerful, with more complication in their working

Figure 3 The Great Eastern Railway had a high level of facilities for their staff. There was even a staff library at Liverpool Street station.

parts. This meant that staff had to have greater knowledge of their machines. In order to train men how to understand and operate the new equipment, the GER built an instruction van. This was converted from a six-wheeled bogie saloon in which the fittings had been removed and replaced with benches, and it had examples of mechanical engine parts as well as a lecture theatre. The van was sent on a tour of the different districts covered by the company.

The use of railways during the war was obviously an important aspect of the conflict. An article in the *Great Eastern Railway Magazine* gave an opinion as to why this was. The GER correspondent was struck most forcibly as to how the present theatre of war was especially suitable for rail transport. There were the gentle undulations of France, the plains of Belgium, and the flat lands of Prussia, while Russia was nothing but a plain. The whole area formed the great central plain of Europe, everywhere less than 600 feet in height offering practically no obstacles to railways.

Chapter 1

1914

The first move in the conflict that became the First World War was the declaration of war between Austria-Hungary and Serbia on 28 July 1914. Russia began to mobilise in support of Serbia. Germany knew they had to move quickly if their plan was to work. Germany declared war on Russia on 1 August and in Britain, preparations were also under way. As early as 30 July, the War Office had given instructions that railway lines were to be guarded. On the Great Western Railway, the line from London to Avonmouth was to be patrolled by platelayers who had to carefully watch bridges and tunnels. There was obviously fear of espionage being carried out on important lines even before Britain became involved in the war.

After the Franco-Prussian War of 1870–71, part of the resulting peace treaty involved the Germans taking control of Luxemburg's railway system, on the stipulation that it was not supposed to be used for military purposes. However, on 1 August, the day Germany declared war on Russia, a truck full of German soldiers arrived at Troisvierges railway station, violating the terms of the treaty. Troisvierges is a small village but, significantly, with a railway line headed towards Belgium.

The Germans tried to take over the telegraph system; they then unbolted some of the rails on the line. This would seem to defeat the object of the plan if they were going to use the railway to move their troops into Belgium. Why pull up the line? The operation does not seem to have been well planned.

Twenty minutes after the German troops arrived, more military vehicles turned up and the soldiers were ordered to leave. This had been the first step in the Schlieffen Plan to invade using the railways. The early invasion of Luxemburg was obviously a mistake and someone had jumped the gun. The German government still had hopes that Britain and even France could still be persuaded to stay out of the war while Germany fought Russia, so the plan was put on hold.

It was soon evident to the Germans that the British were not going to stand by if the Germans invaded France or Belgium. As soon as this became clear, the Schlieffen Plan was put into operation and the next day Luxemburg was again invaded by armoured trains carrying German troops. They were followed by the first of thousands of trains carrying German soldiers towards Belgium.

Michael McDonagh, the parliamentary correspondent of *The Times*, was on the streets of London after Parliament had adjourned on 4 August after war was declared. He said that Parliament Street and Whitehall were 'thronged with people highly excited and rather boisterous. ... All were already touched with war fever', and they regarded their country as the crusader bringing freedom to oppressed nations. Germany was seen as the aggressor and must be made to ask humbly for peace.

Although the Railway Executive Committee had been formed in November 1912 to take control of the railways in the event of war, not everyone involved with the railway system was happy about this. Sir Sam Fay, General Manager of the Great Central Railway, said after the first meeting, 'It was a damned nonsense wasting time over something that will never happen.' He must have been one of the few who could not see the war coming. The committee consisted of the managers of the ten leading railway companies. These were: Sir Frank Ree, London & North Western, (L&NWR); D.A. Matheson, Caledonian; C.H. Dent, Great Northern (GNR); F. Otter, Great Western (GWR); J.A.F. Aspinall, Lancashire & Yorkshire (L&YR); H.A. Walker, London & South Western (L&SWR); Sir Guy Granet, Midland; Sir Sam Fay, Great Central (GCR); Sir A.K. Butterworth, North Eastern (NER); and F.H. Dent, South East & Chatham (SE&CR).

When the war began for Britain on 4 August, the Railway Executive Committee finally took control of the railways. The Railway Executive Committee was chaired by Alexander Kaye Butterworth. The day after war was declared, notice was issued warning the public of difficulties dealing with merchandise, livestock and animals on the railway.

There was some confusion at first as there were differing ideas between railway employees and army officers over what government control meant. Some officers seemed to believe that this meant that the railway system was under martial law. In some cases station masters were arrested and put under armed guard for not doing what they were told.

Figure 4 There were a large number of railway companies at the time of the outbreak of the war. Each company had their own livery and colours. This Great Central locomotive bore the company name as well.

It had to be made clear to some overzealous officers that the railways were under War Office control and that decisions as to the use of trains was dependent on the Army Area Command, not on the whim of any senior officer who wanted to catch a train.

Although the Railway Executive Committee was to take over the railway system, not all the companies were included. There were 130

Figure 5 Great Northern locomotives had the more discreet company initials on the tender.

companies at the time who controlled 98 per cent of Britain's railway mileage. The other 2 per cent were controlled by forty-eight companies, but there were a number of complicated systems in which the companies did not own their own locomotives. These were often run by other companies' engines. These included some electric tramways.

Some of the smaller companies did not come under the control of the Railway Executive Committee. A number of these were obvious ones such as the London Underground lines, which were not included as they carried no goods. However, the Mersey Passenger Railway was. A number of dock railways were also included but the Manchester Ship Canal and railway was not. The Irish railways were to come under separate control in 1916. While the government controlled the railways they guaranteed the level of pre-war profits. This was not a good deal for the railways as they couldn't charge more when they were busy.

The country had been divided into six regional command areas when at war with France in 1793. At the turn of the century there were still six geographic military areas, each with an army corps based there. When the war began each command area was given a Secretary Railway company to arrange the area's military needs. These were: Southern Command – L&SWR; Western Command – L&NWR and Eastern Command – SE&CR (this later changed to the L&NWR); North Command – NER; Scottish Command – NBR (North British Railway); and Irish Command – GNRI (Great Northern Railway of Ireland).

The railways had been busy and had been expanding right up to and into the war. The GCR had recently finished building a new dock system at Immingham, which was mainly for coal exports, although these had stopped immediately war began as all the coal was needed at home. A number of companies had electrification plans, such as the L&NWR, L&YR and the L&SWR. The recent improvements did not benefit the companies financially as they had not existed at the time of the government's guaranteed payments, which were based on 1913 revenue.

The electrification plans were one aspect of the improvements that led to a wartime advantage. Electrification would release steam locomotives for wartime service and, of course, save coal. A number of the electrification schemes involved railways in London such as the L&NWR, and North London Line plans were to run electric trains into Euston and as far out as Watford.

Figure 6 The Tuppenny Tube was the early Underground railway in London and was the first electric underground railway.

The railways were to come into play in the mobilisation of the British forces by carrying the men to the departure points to cross to France. With regard to the large part that the railways played in the war, historian A.J.P. Taylor commented: 'The First World War had begun – imposed on the statesmen of Europe by railway timetables.' He argued that this was due to the powers adhering to pre-existing timetables, especially for the German Schlieffen Plan, and that the trains, once started, must roll remorselessly to their goal. In other words, once the mobilisation began, it could not be stopped, and other countries had to respond or be left behind.

The plans for the mobilisation of the British forces were based on a War Office plan from 1906. This was to involve a force of seven divisions numbering 150,000 men. The actual numbers involved were fewer than this. The plan had one drawback: it had been agreed with France to send the men to France in the event of war. When it came to the real thing, there was disagreement as to where the force would land; there was even consideration of sending them to Germany.

The war began on August bank holiday, when many of the Territorials were still at camp and the railway system was already busy. On the day before war was declared, some Territorials were still on their way to camp and were quickly turned round the following day. However, the extra work of carrying the army to the south coast did not cause too many problems because of all the lines available across different railway companies. There was a lot of choice of routes. The only problems were suffered by the L&SWR as they were working the routes to Southampton.

Not everyone was on the way to France as Territorials did not have to serve abroad. The 271 Brigade Royal Field Artillery Territorials had gone to their annual camp at Lydd in Kent on 26 July. They were ordered to return at a few hours' notice on 2 August and were sent home to wait to be called. On 5 August they were assembled at the Drill Hall in Hornchurch Road, Romford, and there was a move to confiscate local horses to pull their guns. Many of the local carts were left in the street with no horses.

On 7 August, they went to the sidings at Romford station and the horses, guns and equipment were loaded onto a train. The men were loaded onto a separate troop train and they left at midnight, with a large crowd waving them off to war. According to the men, the horrors of war were only realised later by the public. They were not sent to Southampton but were taken to Felixstowe, on the east coast, ready to fight a German invasion if it came.

The Cumbrian Railway had to run twenty-seven trains just to get a unit of Welsh Territorials back home after being instructed to return on the Sunday evening. The L&NWR had to run thirty-three trains to get Territorials home and then take them to their regimental headquarters.

While the army was being moved towards France and the Territorials were being carried home there was a perceived danger to the system. On 15 August, the responsibility for the safety of the railways was taken over by the military. Railways are of course dangerous places and soldiers unfamiliar with the workings had to be told where to stand when on guard duty. This obviously wasn't always adhered to as on the GWR alone, fourteen men were killed by passing trains and two were mistakenly shot by sentries.

The war did have an effect on the normal running of the railways. Some summer excursions cancelled as well as a few passenger trains, but these were soon reinstated. The GER even managed to keep their service from Harwich to the Hook of Holland running throughout the war.

Each company had their own problems but for some, things were slightly easier. The large numbers of troops that came from Aldershot and were taken to Southampton were mainly carried by the L&SWR. In this case there was no need to liaise with other companies. When troops came from further afield, other company trains had to be told when to arrive at the destination from which another company would take the men on to Southampton. If troops were coming from Scotland, for example, they would change in London. So if they came from Scotland on the GNR to London, the L&SWR would be told when to arrive at the London station to carry them on to Southampton.

Many of the troops being sent to France were moved from the north of the country and the trains coming from the north had to pass through London to get to the south coast. The busiest part of London was the North London Line, which was the easiest route for through trains to use.

Figure 7 The first trains taking the British Army to the war were well attended by the soldiers' families to see them off. The war was seen as an exciting adventure by the public and the soldiers.

The Metropolitan Line was also very useful. The company had installed steam-operated widened lines in 1866, which had given the GNR and the Midland access to the city. This line led to the connections of the GNR line to Kent, and so to Dover. The gradients on the line did not make the running of so many trains easy. The steepest gradients were in the tunnels for southbound trains.

The number of men on each train was quite low at about 200 men per train. The British troops travelled in relative comfort on this side of the Channel. Once they reached France things were often much less comfortable. Many of them travelled in horseboxes. In Continental reasoning, five men equalled one horse when it came to filling their trucks.

One of the first units to arrive in France was the seven-platoon B Company of the second battalion of the South Staffordshire Regiment. They were commanded by Second Lieutenant Arnold Gyde. After they arrived at Le Havre they were taken to the station to board a train. Gyde said that despite the transport consisting of cattle trucks, the men were in such high spirits that this did not dampen them. In fact, the men were imitating the sounds of cattle and sheep as they boarded. Some of the

Figure 8 British troops arriving in France. These were luckier than many as they were on a passenger train, not in horseboxes.

trucks had instructions printed on them stating capacity for eight horses or forty men.

War often led to rumours and strange tales but perhaps one of the strangest was the belief that 300,000 Russian troops had arrived at a northern port in Britain and were secretly carried on trains with the blinds drawn. They were supposedly carried down to the south and sent across to France. It seemed that everyone knew someone who had seen the trains and, of course, the Russians still had snow on their boots!

There is little doubt that the large armies that had been built up by those taking part in the war had to be moved and that railway transport was the means by which this happened. This was especially true of the German Army, who were moved across land. They had developed schedules that led to concentrations of troops at depots, which meant that they could be sent to where they were needed. The German railways had been made in peacetime but to serve the country in the purpose of war. The advantages of this had been realised after the use of railways in the American Civil War and the Franco-Prussian War – experience that seems to have been used by the Germans but not by the French to the same level. The successful use of the railways in the war of 1870–71 between France and Germany had been a major reason for the Germans' rapid victory. This had enabled them to quickly put an army of nearly half a million men on the French frontier to face a French army of half that size. The German use of railways once again put them in a prime position.

At the time of the Franco-Prussian war a single line track could carry eight trains a day; a double track could carry twelve. By the outbreak of the First World War, these numbers had increased to forty and sixty, enabling many more troops and equipment to move quickly. Despite the German planning, they were never able to succeed in their intent to surround Paris very quickly and force the French to surrender; instead, they ended up being bogged down in a trench war.

The Germans were the leaders in this type of movement of men and their Schlieffen Plan meant that they could send their troops to the borders of their country very quickly. They expected the Russians to be very slow to mobilise in the east and progressed quickly through Belgium and into Northern France, which would, they hoped, lead to a quick surrender by the French, leaving the Germans to then deal with the Russians.

There is a train of thought that war was inevitable once one country had mobilised. This idea was that once Russia began to mobilise, Germany had to follow, and once started, it couldn't be stopped in case other countries mobilised and led the way. This argument was from a military point of view. The German Army had begun to prepare the railways in July and the railway in Luxemburg was important to their plan. They were then going to sweep through Belgium and into France.

It was the use of the railways that eventually foiled the German plan when the Belgians sabotaged much of their system and delayed the German advance. The German Army included ninety companies of railway troops to fix any problems they encountered. They did not anticipate, however, that the Belgians would do so much damage to their own railway system. They also did not take into account how serious damage to delicate signalling systems would be.

Although the Germans did reach France quickly, the damage to Belgium's railways meant that the German supply lines were severely

Figure 9 German troops on a train. They look quite composed, perhaps being used to railway travel in wartime.

curtailed. In some cases there was an 80-mile gap between German forces and the railways being used to supply them. The Germans also made a mistake in placing too much emphasis on cavalry, as horses were much more difficult to transport. It soon became clear that mounted troops were of little use in a modern war, and they took up much of the capacity of rail transport. The number of trains needed to carry 4,000 cavalry could carry 16,000 infantry.

It wasn't only in Europe that the German plans for railways were put forward and in one case it was not the French but the British that German plans threatened. The Germans had proposed a Berlin to Baghdad railway line with a branch extending to Basra. This was very close to India, which the British had always tried to protect from other European powers; the danger to India from Russia had been a historical threat but they were now allies.

The German line was never actually finished but the threat was yet another basis for putting two European powers in conflict with each other. It also led to German co-operation with the Ottoman Empire, which resulted in conflict between Britain and Turkey.

Meanwhile, the French were using their railway system to move their forces to oppose the Germans. The French had also carried out sabotage to their own railway system close to the German border. In addition, they had been working to improve their railway system because of the historic threat from Germany. New sidings had been added to many of the German stations located on the borders of France and Belgium. In reply, the French built new stations with very long platforms to allow longer trains to be used.

There was another big difference between the two nations in that the German government controlled a number of the railways in Germany. In France, however, as in Britain, the railways were privately owned.

Despite the carefully planned German tactics they didn't lead to the success they had hoped for. Within France and Belgium they had problems supplying the troops they had managed to get in place so quickly. They had also expected a swift success in Russia, hoping to defeat them before they could mobilise. Although the Russian system may not have been as up to date as those of its European rivals, it still enabled them to mobilise much more quickly than the Germans had expected.

The Germans moved forward so fast that there were not enough railways working to supply them because of the damage done by the Belgians to their own railway system. When the German troops pulled back because of the problems with getting supplies to the positions they had reached, the French then had to repair their own railways that they had previously sabotaged so they could now send their troops forward. It soon became evident that it was the defenders who had the advantage as the advancing army needed secure supply routes that could move with them.

There was also a great difference in the reliability of the railway services of each of the main protagonists. In Germany, the military mainly ran the railways and did so very well. France had a mixed system of military and public railways, which didn't always run well together. Russia had the worst system and had to be sent 875 locomotives from America and Canada over the course of the war as they were so short of equipment. These were mainly 2-10-0 locomotives but the Russian Revolution that began in 1917 meant that not all of these were delivered as America and

Figure 10 Henry J. Spencer, a member of the RE railway department. Spencer would most likely have had a railway background. It was quite common for soldiers to have their images produced as postcards.

European nations became wary of the new Communist government. The British system was privately owned but there was also a military railway force, which was to grow during the war.

Britain's railway troops were trained at Longmoor in Hampshire, which had originally been the Woolmer Instructional Military Railway. The railway troops under the Royal Engineers had been based at Chattenden until 1905 but then moved to Longmoor. Most of the railway troops that went to France and other areas of conflict trained there and the engines at the site were given names. In 1914, they received a second-hand 0-6-2T locomotive called *Thisbe*. It came from the Shropshire and Montgomeryshire Light Railway. It then went to Rhyl as WD 84.

At the outbreak of war there were only two regular and three Reserve Royal Engineers railway companies. These were the Eighth Railway Company, Tenth Railway Company, the Depot Company, Royal Anglesey Company and the Royal Monmouth Company. The Eighth went to France in August to help maintain the rail networks that were in Allied hands.

The repairs that had to be carried out to damaged railway lines in the battle areas led to a great demand for skilled workers to join the British railway-operating troops. This was an obvious need and recruitment was organised by William Forbes, later Sir William, General Manager of the London, Brighton & South Coast Railway (LBSCR), and Lieutenant Colonel Commandant of the Engineering and Railway Staff Corps, an advisory body. He enlisted the first men and formed the first sections of the new companies.

Later, Mr A. Watson, Superintendent of the Line of the L&YR, undertook the enrolment of the Transport Corps, RE, the labour troops, and Army Service Corps. He also organised the Military Forwarding Establishment, which moved goods too large for the army postal service to the front.

The involvement of railway company officers in military matters was a common occurence early in the war. Sir Francis Dent, General Manager of SE&CR, was a lieutenant colonel in the Engineer and Railway Staff Corps. He also began to work on the Operating Corps. There were early problems involving pay, the form of enrolment and the qualifications of applicants. These were eventually dealt with by a subcommittee of the Railway Executive Committee.

Figure 11 When German troops tried to reach France by train they found many of the Belgian railways had been sabotaged, as shown in this image.

The influence that railwaymen had on the military during the war is one that is often overlooked. Men such as Dent, Forbes and Watson were just a small section of the managers and technical experts employed on the railways who also played such a huge part in the military branch of the railway service that was to prove so vital for the war effort. It is most often the young men who went to the front and fought who are the ones who are remembered and commemorated. However, these were older men and although they had some military experience, it was their railway experience that made them so vital. It was their knowledge and understanding of the railway system that helped keep the British forces on the front line equipped with the enormous numbers of supplies that were needed to fight the war.

The need to enlist the correct railwaymen for these military duties was paramount. There were cases of men being sent back to their former employers as they were not qualified to do the work required. It was because of this need for the right men that enlistment for the military railway units was made through the general managers of the railway companies. It was due to their specialised knowledge that many of the men they put forward were capable of a much higher grade of work than they had been carrying out for the railway companies. This was often tested out before they moved to a military unit.

After receiving military training some of the recruits were returned to their civil employment for a period. They were then called for as needed for service overseas. Many of the officers for the military railway troops were also ex-railway employees. Those who were called up were often replaced by retired men being brought back or by women where it was thought the work was suitable for them.

Although there were women working on the railways when the war broke out they were not doing the type of jobs that one may expect. As already mentioned, cleaning and waitressing were obvious roles but others that may have seemed ideal for women at that time, such as clerks, were not. The role of clerk had been a strictly male occupation on the railway, but of course this had to change when Kitchener called for more men.

Figure 12 A group of female railway workers at Luton. Although the first women who worked on the railways did mainly lighter work, they later took over the much more strenuous roles that had previously been performed by men. This group looks as though they are responsible for maintenance.

The Germans may have been swift to use the railway system to get their men in place but the British were not far behind in being so organised, although they had fewer men to carry – as the Kaiser was quick to point out with his comment on their 'contemptible little army'. Consequently, the British forces that were first into France became known as 'The Old Contemptibles'.

The *Great Eastern Railway Magazine* described how, in early August, the regular troops were spread around the country in barracks and camps – from Land's End to John O'Groats. This led to the greatest task that the railway had ever faced. All stations were fed with men making for mobilisation centres. Meanwhile, the railway system still carried the general public to work and to whatever other destinations they wanted to travel to. Up until the outbreak of war many of the population were still planning holidays, including to destinations on the Continent. Advice given by the railway companies was that it might be best to put off holiday plans until winter. There was obviously still the belief that it would all be over by Christmas and those European routes could then restart.

The article went on to say that railways in wartime were like a large torpedo tube that discharged armies at vital points on the enemy lines. Britain's railway companies were obviously up to the task, as Earl Kitchener said to the House of Lords on 25 August: 'The railway companies in the all-important matter of the transport facilities have more than justified the complete confidence reposed in them by the War Office, all grades of railway services having laboured with untiring energy and patience.'

The movement of troops was organised by the Army Area Commands and their secretary companies. The way the railways were normally run did not apply in the case of troop trains. They had to work out timetables from the destinations backwards. This was a War Office directive as the troops had to arrive at the right time so that their baggage could be loaded onto the correct ships to accompany them.

With the organisation of the trains, there had to be different forms of transport available. This would include first class coaches for officers and seated accommodation for the rest of the men. This was to be at a level of comfort that many of the men would not experience once they crossed the Channel, after which they could find themselves being transported in horseboxes. The cattle trucks this side of the Channel were for horses. Luggage trucks would be needed to carry all the baggage.

Figure 13 Troops arriving in France – again, lucky to have been carried on passenger trains.

Organising the trains would only be the start of the process. Depending on where the train originated from, it would have to be ascertained whether it could be pulled all the way by a single locomotive or have to be changed for one from another company en route. There was also the problem of whether the train could manage the loading gauge of any other railway companies' lines that it would pass through. If the train drivers had to drive over unknown lines then pilot drivers would have to assist them.

It was not only the welfare of the soldiers that had to be dealt with during the journey. If the locomotive staff had to spend the night away from home then they had to have somewhere to stay and they had to be fed. It would also have to be established if there was anything that could be brought back to avoid the train returning empty.

There was an interesting comment published in the *War Illustrated Magazine* on women working during the conflict. A women worker said that her husband had been one of the first to go abroad with the

Expeditionary Force in August 1914. The woman's husband was against her going to work while he was away. He said that she was already paid the government separation allowance and if she took a job she may be doing someone else out of employment who needed the money more. Perhaps it was more the case that men did not like their wives going out to work. For some men this seemed to threaten their position as the breadwinner.

Money was obviously one of the important factors when the family breadwinner went off to war. The GER were quick to realise this and the front cover of their magazine in September tried to allay these fears for their staff. A message from H.W. Thornton, the General Manager, explained that the wives and families of men volunteering for the forces as well as those reservists being called up would be given allowances by the company. These would be supplemented by personal contributions made by the directors, officers and staff so that with the government pay there would be sufficient money for the families' maintenance for the time the men spent with the colours. I doubt if anyone suspected how long this would be or how much these allowances would eventually amount to.

Many of the men who moved from the civil railways to the military railways found themselves in an unusual position. In many cases the railway troops were not officially part of the regular or the Territorial forces. This led to some disadvantages as they did not benefit from the collections for comforts organised for ordinary troops. There were therefore separate collections for them amongst railway staff. The money raised by the public exhibition of ambulance trains also added to this fund. What may seem insignificant items such as underclothes, footballs and pipes were often a means of raising the men's morale.

An example of this was given by Lieutenant Charles Travis of the GCR. Travis was serving in the forces but was engaged in special railway duties at home. He described the provision for soldiers passing through Perth station by an organisation known as 'Perthshire Patriotic Barrow'. They would give out drinks and fruit to men on trains passing through. This was obviously a great help when refreshments were not always available to the men while travelling. They also helped any men in difficulties and provided what was available for any man in need.

Although many railwaymen went on to serve in a similar capacity in the forces, some carried out a very different form of service, often with spectacular results. J.E. Curtis was a railway police constable for the Midland Railway. He was a naval reservist and became a second class petty officer in the Royal Navy when the war began. He was awarded the Russian Medal of the Order of St Anna by no less a personage than the Czar. This was earned while serving in the White Sea. Curtis had served in the navy before his railway employment and already held the China Medal from his previous service. Such events were widely reported in the various railway magazines, which looked for any opportunity to report on the success of their employees in the forces.

In England, ships were waiting for the men who would cross to France, mainly at Southampton, but they had to be carried from various barracks spread around the country. By the end of August, the railway had transported almost 120,000 men to Southampton. They had also carried nearly 40,000 horses, more than 300 guns, over 5,000 vehicles, 1,800 bicycles and nearly 5,000 tons of baggage. Once the British troops

Figure 14 Docks were important in the war both for sending and receiving goods and men. Many were owned by railway companies. This image shows Falmouth and the close rail line used to move goods to and from the dock.

reached France they were dependent on travelling on the French railway system and this did not always match the comfort they had enjoyed on trains before crossing the Channel.

There were six divisions of infantry and one of cavalry ready to fight when the war broke out. Of these, four infantry divisions and the cavalry division went to France. The movement of the British Expeditionary Force (BEF) was mainly the responsibility of the L&SWR, who oversaw the London Command. They then instructed other companies as to when troops had to arrive at which junctions and at what time. All the troop trains were marked with an X and a number.

1Daily News described the movement of troops as a wonderful achievement done in the light of flares and arc lamps, with not one man or horse injured. Whether this was an exaggeration or not isn't clear; it seems feasible that with all the men and equipment being loaded and moved there must have been some injuries even if they were only slight, but the morale of the public was as important as that of the troops. The BEF fought their first battle at Mons on 23 August, just two weeks after the movement of troops to the Continent had begun.

The movement of troops around the country saw attempts to provide the men with refreshments on their journey. In mid-August, free refreshments were given to troops in some locations at the railway stations. This soon began to spread to other areas, where volunteers would hand out fruit to the men as the trains stopped at certain points. Tea would also be provided. This was mainly the work of volunteers but the Red Cross also began to help.

The soldiers who were sent across to France in the first days of the war were regulars. For new volunteers things were not so clear cut. There were often restrictions on the movement of men who had enlisted. Some were sent home after they joined up because there were no quarters ready for them. In many cases, there were no weapons or uniforms for new recruits either.

Catching a train, however, wasn't easy for those who did have uniforms who were sent home. Many stations were guarded by the Military Police and a soldier had to have a leave pass to enable him to buy a ticket, which was not always supplied. One way round this was to go to a small village station and quickly show an old leave pass that the ticket clerk might not examine too closely. New recruits were not as wise as experienced men in the ways of bending the rules.

Many of the early volunteers were men from the railway companies. There were later some attempts to slow down the rate of railway workers enlisting as it would seriously affect the running of the service. The London Underground, for instance, lost many men to enlistment – as many as 2,500 in the first months of the war. Despite the need for railway workers to remain in their civilian posts, another 2,000 London railway employees enlisted over the course of the war.

Getting the men to France was only the beginning. The general work of the railways still had to be done and was evident in places such as the Caledonian Railway area where there were thirty large engineering works, forty-three iron and steel works and thirty-five shipbuilding works. The company also needed to take coal to the fleet based in their area. Some of the gradients on their lines were so steep that they needed help with extra engines to pull the trains. In August alone, 342 naval or military trains were carried on their system.

If the situation seemed busy for the Caledonian Railway in the first months of the war, it was soon to become much busier. At the time when war broke out, there had been two explosive works in their area – the

Figure 15 A Somerset and Dorset Railway locomotive. The S&DR was one of the smaller companies still in existence during the war.

Figure 16 A Caledonian Railways locomotive. The Caledonian was not one of the largest companies but played a full part in the war, supplying coal to the British fleet at Scapa Flow.

Roslin Glenn Gunpowder Mill in Midlothian and Nobel's Explosives – but by the end of the war there were seven. There were also many military camps being set up, which, along with the munitions works, needed new sidings to be built. The company's own workshops were also producing gun carriages and water tank carts, and they converted sixteen coaches for ambulance trains.

Once the first wave of troops reached France, there was a lull in proceedings. September saw a return to almost normality in the business of running the railways for their regular passengers. Private excursions were restarted and even some traffic to the Continent for the general public continued. The LB&SCR were continuing to run the Newhaven to Dieppe crossing. The SE&CR timetable still showed the Continental services but with a note that the trains were liable to be altered or even withdrawn. Other companies were less able to carry on with this service; the GER had problems with Continental routes as several of its ships had been commandeered by the Admiralty.

The early ambulance trains were not the specially designed and built models of the later part of the war, which were constructed to the latest specifications. The first GER ambulance train was described as a 'striking instance of ingenious adaption of rolling stock'. The nine vehicles of the train had not been specially built for the purpose. They were withdrawn from the modern bogie stock and altered to War Office plans. Five of the coaches were brake thirds, two were main line composites, one was a brake and luggage van, and the last was a first class dining car. The five brake thirds were ward cars with twenty beds each; the luggage van was a pharmacy and operating theatre; and the two composites were accommodation for medical staff. As the war progressed and the weaponry developed, so did medical care.

Railway workshops also played a huge part in the war effort. The GER Works at Stratford in East London was employing more than 6,000 workers when the war began. In 1912, they built thirty-nine locomotives, including the first five S69 LNER B12 4-6-0s. They also built eighty-two new carriages and seventy-five non-passenger vehicles, including an elephant van. When the war began the site undertook munitions work, including building one of the hospital trains for the army. Even before they took on the military work, they had already been hard-pressed to manage the volume of work for the GER. The government agreed to their request to be allowed to build a new locomotive repair facility, and this opened the following year. Not all war work involved munitions and railway equipment. The works also built six henhouses for the GER farm at Bentley in Suffolk.

Wolverton Railway Works in Buckinghamshire belonged to the London and Birmingham Railway but this later became part of the L&NWR. In 1901 it became the first railway workshop to use electricity for lighting and operating machinery. During the war, carriages were altered there to turn them into ambulance vehicles for use at home and overseas. Part of the works was also taken over by the Ministry of Munitions.

In 1914, Wolverton was employing 5,000 workers, although many of the men soon enlisted in the forces and, as was the case at other workshops, they were replaced by women. Some of the ambulance trains made at Wolverton were paid for by public subscription and members of the public were allowed to inspect them before they were put into use. This was to become a common event later in the war and was often a means of raising money as an entrance fee was charged.

One of the trains built at the workshop was a very special job with many modern conveniences. It was equipped with a telephone, a generator and

R. & W. HAWTHORN LESLIE & Co., LTD.,

FORTH BANKS WORKS
NEWCASTLE-ON-TYNE

MANUFACTURERS OF LOCOMOTIVES
OF EVERY DESCRIPTION FOR HOME
AND FOREIGN RAILWAYS.

ESTABLISHED 1817.

COMBINED CRANES AND TANK
LOCOMOTIVES ALWAYS IN STOCK
& IN PROGRESS FOR COLLIERIES,
IRONWORKS, RAILWAY DEPOTS,
BRANCH LINES CONTRACTORS.
ETC.

TELEGRAPHIC ADDRESS:
"LOCOMOTIVE, NEWCASTLE-ON-TYNE."

Figure 17 An advertisement for a railway engineering company. Such companies were ideally set up for the heavy engineering work needed for war supplies.

a boiler for heating and hot water. There were ten carriages converted from picnic saloons. It was used by Sir Douglas Haig, the Commander-in-Chief in France, as his mobile headquarters.

The main objective of the railways at this time may have been to move men to France but there were also some passengers coming the other way. Early in September, a train arrived at Liverpool Street station carrying British refugees from Germany. They had been taken from Berlin to the Hook of Holland and crossed on the SS *Copenhagen*. The refugees had been given very short notice and so found it difficult to get passports and luggage ready. Despite the difficulties, they were the lucky ones; many other British civilians later found themselves interned in Germany in retaliation for the internment of German civilians in Britain.

The passengers were met by the Lord Mayor of London and the Mayor of Westminster, and they had various tales to tell. Some had been treated very well by the Germans whilst others had a number of complaints. One lady claimed that German officers, noblemen all, had turned British visitors and servants out onto the streets. She had been forced to report to a police station daily and if she was late, the police would come looking for her.

There was a wave of anti-German feeling spreading across Britain when the war began, which soon escalated into violence. There were attacks on shops owned by citizens with German-sounding names. There were even cases of parents with such names being attacked while their children were serving in the British forces. In some areas there was anti-German rioting, often if not inspired by, but supported by certain sections of the press. The beginning of internment of those seen as enemy aliens was, in part, a move by the government to protect them from attack rather than because they were a danger to the country.

The anti-German feeling sweeping the country also had an effect on the railways. In November, the L&NWR 4-6-0 Experiment class locomotive named *Germanic* had new nameplates fitted. It was now called *Belgic*. The old nameplates on the driving wheel splashers were left in place but the names were crossed out. The GWR Star class locomotive

Figure 18 An aged-looking GWR locomotive. Many older railway vehicles that may otherwise have been scrapped remained in use during the war.

No. 4017 called *Knight of the Black Eagle* was renamed *Knight of Liege*. The Black Eagle was an ancient Prussian chivalry order.

The movement of British troops to the Continent left the railway system in the UK as what the French called the 'Zone of the Interior'. The railway system had to be protected so that it was capable of supplying goods to the army abroad and carrying reinforcements to them. It was also a vital means of home defence in the event of an invasion attempt by the Germans.

The serious anti-German feeling continued to run through the country. There were many people from German backgrounds residing in the UK as large numbers of German immigrants had arrived in the late nineteenth century. Many of these had been aiming to get to America but for one reason or another had got as far as the UK and stopped. It was also believed that there were large numbers of German spies in the country and that many of the Germans living here were part of this group.

There was a belief that Germany had a means of mapping the more vulnerable points of the railway system in countries that they planned to invade and this would seem to have been based on experience of their use of railways in the countries they had already occupied. A question often asked was, why did German barbers always have their businesses near railway stations? Perhaps it was because they were likely to be where they would get passing trade, but more sinister beliefs abounded.

For these reasons it was thought necessary to guard vulnerable points on the railways such as tunnels, junctions, bridges and remote signal boxes. This was at first carried out by railway employees, often supported by the police and even Boy Scouts. It was evident, however, that these guards were not going to be able to deter a serious German saboteur, so the government decided that Territorials should take over the job.

There was an attempt to prioritise the most important lines, such as those used for troop movements both for abroad and for home defence. The lines were graded in order of priority and those thought to be the most important were guarded by armed soldiers. The less important could still be watched by the previous amateur guardians.

Of course, one of the most memorable legacies of the First World War is that it inspired a wave of young poets who were mainly serving officers and whose poems were based on the futility or the sadness of war. They are remembered as the War Poets, with famous names such as Siegfried

Figure 19 Civilians were the first to guard the railways but were soon replaced by the military. This image shows a Canadian soldier guarding a tunnel, although the overgrown tracks suggest it was not a busy line.

Sassoon, Wilfred Owen and others still very much in the forefront of poetry today.

There was one poet with strong railway connections who was not a serving officer as he had failed the medical for the army. His poems were not about the horrors or the futility of war but were very anti-German, and due to the attitude in the country at the time were well received.

Henry Chappell was a porter for the GWR at Bath station. He had previously published poems about railway journeys such as the first non-stop London to Plymouth run in 1903. In August 1914, Chappell wrote an anti-German poem called *The Day*, which was published in the

Daily Express – a strongly anti-German newspaper. It is hard to imagine any newspaper today publishing such a poem. It described the Germans as 'Blasphemer, braggart and coward all'. In fact, it reflected the feelings of many people in Britain after stories of German soldiers killing babies in Belgium became widespread. Propaganda became a weapon encouraged by many of the best-known writers of the period so perhaps the success of Chappell's poem is no surprise.

The poem was even known in America, and Chappell was complimented on his work by no lesser person than Rudyard Kipling, who visited him at Bath. The instant fame led to Chappell having a book of poems published. It was claimed that he made £100 from *The Day* and that he donated it all to the Red Cross. Despite the fame and popularity his work aroused at the time, Chappell was never one of the best-remembered war poets.

Although Continental services carried on through the early months of the war, the dangers were clear. The last GER ship left Antwerp in early October – only two days before the Germans took the city. The company then moved the service to Ostend, where a number of British railway ships tried to clear the large crowds of refugees and travellers before the Germans arrived again in the middle of October.

The movement of the refugees once they disembarked in Dover and Folkestone was one of the biggest challenges faced by the SE&CR. In one day in mid-October they ran eight special trains taking the refugees to reception centres around the country. The GER, having lost their base at Harwich to the navy, ran services taking refugees to Tilbury.

On one day, 6,000 refugees from Ostend were landed at Folkestone, many of them with nothing but the clothes they wore. The SE&CR not only had to transport them, they also had to feed them, find them somewhere to stay and then move them to somewhere they could be given permanent accommodation.

Many of the refugees arriving in the country were from Belgium. Some of these were to be useful to the war effort. Men of military age were expected to join a Belgian military unit. Some, such as Belgian railway workers, had other useful skills. The Railway Executive Committee opened an office in Westminster, where the refugee railwaymen were directed into work suitable to their skills. They were ideal replacements for the railwaymen who had gone to join the military.

Figure 20 Folkestone was to see the arrival of many refugees from occupied Europe, mainly Belgians.

The L&NWR was one of the more important contributors to the war effort. They ran trains from Euston to the Scottish west coast. This meant that much of the traffic from the north was carried by them to London, where the North London Line became one of the main links with the south. Crossing London from the north to the south was always a problem. The L&NWR were the secretary company for the South Command, such was their importance.

The schedule delays that were a consequence of the outbreak of war soon settled back to normal after the BEF had left for France. Most of the railway companies had resumed their regular service by September, except for the LSWR, who were still busy with military work and took another week to get back to normal. Many trains were then crowded as the public set off on delayed holidays. A number of extra trains ran to cope with the demands of the public, who were not going to be denied a holiday by the small matter of a war.

Sir Frank Ree, the L&NWR General Manager, had played a leading part in the negotiations with the War Office and the Board of Trade that had led to the formation of the Railway Executive Committee. Many of the railway companies' general managers played a part in this, as well as in other aspects of the conflict later in the war.

The company improved connections with a number of other company lines, especially around London, as well as building numerous new sidings at munitions and other factories producing war work. Many of the L&NWR's old carriages became homes and sentry boxes for railway guards at strategic points as the railway system was seen as a primary target for saboteurs.

The Midland Railway works at Derby had been employing 40,000 people at the turn of the century, making about forty locomotives a year. As with other workshops, they turned to producing weapons for the government. They produced eleven howitzers by the end of the 1914. They then began to produce shells and their component parts. At first they produced 3,000 fuses a week but after installing automated machines, they turned out many times that number.

During the war, the Derby works still produced locomotives for the Midland and the GNR. They also made some for the Somerset and

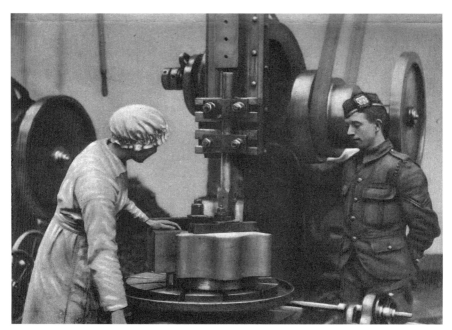

Figure 21 Railway workshops were important in producing armaments and as the war progressed, much of the work was undertaken by women.

Dorset Joint Railway, which included some heavy freight 2-8-0s. They built these in batches during and after the war. They also built a number of 0-6-0s.

The Midland ran from their base at Derby to Carlisle in the north, Manchester and Liverpool in the west, and Lincoln in the east. Like many other railway companies, they had their own port, at Heysham in Lancashire. The industrial areas covered by the company had a total of 258 munitions works; ninety-seven of these were new and had been set up since the start of hostilities. The company had problems later in the war in providing suitable vehicles for special work such as carrying aircraft and tanks.

The Midland also had an interest in lines much further south, where they controlled the London, Tilbury and Southend line, which had been in competition for routes with the GER. The rivalry was so fierce that it led to refusal to allow trains from one company to use the other's station. At Romford in Essex there were separate stations on the same site. The Midland would use this southern line as part of the route for carrying mines from Scotland to Dagenham Dock and large guns to the artillery testing camp at Shoeburyness.

When the war began, there were 13,000 women working on the railway but this soon changed as the numbers of women working in transport quickly reached 100,000. Many of these were employed on the railways but they were by this time taking on traditional male roles. More than 1.5 million women took on male roles in industry during the war and what was even more shocking was that they wore trousers!

The outbreak of war led to an increase in work for the railway companies but this was in relation to the conflict. The development of the railway system was in other ways put on hold. There had been plans in 1914 for linking the North Wales narrow gauge railway with the Porthmadog, Beddgelert and South Snowdon Railway to make a through route. This was one of the plans put on hold.

The L&SWR had been important to the British military for a long period before the war. Their lines covered the military and naval areas of Salisbury Plain, Weymouth, Plymouth, Portsmouth and Aldershot. It was already known as 'England's military Line' before the war had begun. It had been responsible for carrying almost all the troops involved in the Boer War to their disembarkation points.

The company had owned the port at Southampton since 1892 and had spent a lot of money improving services there. The government then took it over without having spent a penny. The port included 37 miles of railway lines within it. During the war the port was as good as closed to public use. At its busiest there were 100 troop-carrying trains arriving each day.

There were 176 army camps close to Southampton, all of which were on L&SWR lines. The majority of these camps had railway sidings running to the camps from main lines. Many of these lines had been laid by the military using equipment provided by the L&SWR but these were then run by the company. The company also were responsible for laying another 3 miles of sidings at Eastleigh.

As well as men being sent from Southampton to France, they also came back from there, many of them on hospital trains. Although the majority of these men were then taken to hospitals around the country, some didn't have as far to go. At the north-east side of Southampton Water stood the Royal Victoria Hospital. The Royal Victoria was the British Army's first purpose-built hospital. Constructed during the Crimean War, it had more than 100 wards and 1,000 beds.

The hospital had its own pier so that the wounded could be landed direct from ships, but it was never built long enough to reach the deep water and smaller boats had to be used to carry the patients from the ships. The problem was solved when a railway line was built to the hospital from Southampton Docks. The pier, known as Netley Pier, was then used for recreation by the patients. Many of the wounded seen on the pier in the First World War were from the tented wards added to increase the hospital's capacity.

Many of the very small railways still in existence played a part in the war. The Hundred of Manhood and Selsey Tramway was actually a light railway. It was called a tramway to get round the regulations faced by a railway that did not apply to tramways. It ran between Chichester and Selsey and although it only had one line, this was known as the Chichester to Selsey section. There had been plans to build a branch line to Wittering but this never happened.

The line had eleven stations or halts, but no signals, and had six level crossings, some on busy roads, but had no gates or warning system for them. The guard had to get off the train before the crossing and hold

Figure 22 Many small light railways played a part in the war. This line to Coryton in the Essex marshes carried workers and supplies to a munitions factory on the banks of the Thames.

up traffic with a red flag. With army barracks and the First World War Graylingwell Hospital at Chichester, there must have been a number of military passengers using the tramway.

There were a number of light railways in operation before and during the war. Many of these served industries such as quarrying and, especially, mining. The lines into the sites were often seen as sidings to the main railway that they connected to. Light railways to places such as coal mines were obviously very busy.

Meanwhile, war requirements were taking precedence over public use of the railways. One of the services now provided by the railway companies was building special ambulance trains. The use of ambulance and invalid carriages pre-dated the war. The L&SWR, for instance, had two invalid carriages built at Eastleigh in 1910. These carriages had six armchairs, a couch, a luggage compartment, a four-seat first class compartment, a six-seat third class compartment and a toilet.

The first wartime ambulance trains were of nine coaches but the number of coaches was later increased. They were usually adapted from existing stock. The later ones were very long – up to sixteen carriages – so that they could carry as many wounded soldiers as possible, and were specially built. The carriages were overcrowded, having three tiers of bunk beds so they could carry as many wounded men as possible. Officers were usually kept separate from other ranks and were treated much better – a common practice in most military railway services.

The trains carried their own supplies of drugs and medical equipment. There were operating theatres, kitchens and accommodation for the staff. The doctors and nurses often worked through the night while risking catching disease and lice, and in danger from being bombed. The men coming straight from the trenches were also often dirty and smelly. The patients suffered the same risks, and despite the relief of moving away from the front, it could be a painful experience for the wounded, who could feel every bump as the train moved.

The GCR built three ambulance trains, the GER two, GWR four, the L&YR two, the L&NWR five, the L&SWR two and the Midland Railway two. There were also five naval ambulance trains built at Wolverton from August 1914. Four of these had twelve coaches. The other one only had seven coaches as it was for use in the steep gradients

Figure 23 Ambulance trains were built by many of the railway companies, usually to a similar design, such as this one belonging to the GWR.

of Scotland, where parts of the fleet were based. Some of these remained in use after the war.

The ambulance trains were used at home but were also used overseas. The first ambulance trains to arrive home carrying the wounded were greeted by large crowds and often a band. It soon became evident to those watching that there was little to celebrate when they saw the seriously hurt men that the trains were carrying. Many of the men were in no mood to rejoice.

The number of different railway companies still in operation during the war led to a wider variety of locomotives in use. One of these was a 4-4-4 wheel base system that although more common in places like America, was quite rare in Britain. In the late nineteenth century, the Wirral Railway, the Midland and South Western Railway, the North Eastern Railway and the Metropolitan Railway had these types of locomotives; three of them were made by Beyer Peacock.

The most numerous examples of 4-4-4s were the Sir Vincent Raven class D, with a three-cylinder system. Raven was chief mechanical engineer of the NER from 1910 to 1922. These engines were built for the NER from 1913, originally for the Darlington Line. They were later rebuilt as 4-6-2s.

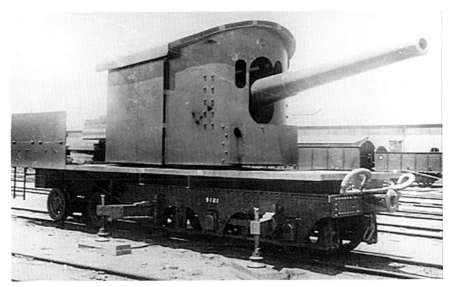

Figure 24 A large, well-protected army gun mounted on a railway truck, South West Africa, c. 1915. (*British Government photograph in the Australian War Memorial archive/ Wikimedia Commons*)

The conflict was of course taking place overseas but there was always a danger of an enemy landing or a raid in Britain, and one of the areas of concern that needed guarding were the railways. The military, however, were needed elsewhere. There were still members of the armed forces at home who could do this job. There were also a number of men working on the railways with previous military and firearms experience. Arming these men would have released troops for other duties and of course, railway employees would have a much keener sense of what was in danger on their home turf than inexperienced military men.

The War Office was not interested in the idea of squads of civilian marksmen guarding the railways. Their view was that every able-bodied man who could shoot should be enlisting in the forces. There were many men whose occupation meant that they could not enlist and these were a resource that could have been of use in such situations.

The available men were the National Reserve and they took over railway guard duties from October. These were men who were over the age for serving abroad but who had volunteered for military jobs at home. Railway employees also helped to guard important junctions and tunnels where there was no military presence, which usually included less important military lines.

The firearms experience of many railwaymen was due to them having previous military experience. Railway jobs were often the chosen occupation of ex-military and naval men, as is demonstrated in the rolls of honour of railwaymen who died early in the war. Gunner J. Adams had only been employed by the GER since March 1914 after leaving the army. As a reservist he was called up on 4 August and died on 13 September. Albert Isaacs had been employed by the GER since 1908 after spending twelve years in the navy. He was also a reservist and was called up on 3 August. Isaacs was a crew member on the HMS *Hogue* and lost his life on 22 September when his ship was one of three sunk by a German submarine in the North Sea. Another GER employee, Mr W. Nichols, who had also been employed since 1908, was called up as a naval reserve and was a crew member on the HMS *Aboukir*, another ship that was sunk on 22 September.

By October, things were not going well for the Allies in Belgium, especially at Antwerp. The railways were trying to support the troops and there were two armoured trains running on the system in Antwerp,

F. FOSTER, porter, Traffic Department, Evesham.

W. HITCHCOCK, stower, Goods Department, Smithfield.

G. T. WOODS, carriage fitter, Locomotive and Carriage Dept., Old Oak Common.

A. C. CROCKER, riveter's assistant, Locomotive and Carriage Dept., Wormwood Scrubbs.

W. H. KING, messenger, Goods Department, Bristol.

W. H. FINCKEN, porter, Goods Department, Paddington.

A. W. EDWARDS porter, Goods Department, Hockley.

R. DRURY, shed porter, Goods Department, Cardiff.

A. H. COLLENS, porter, Traffic Department, Grange Court.

W. E. AYLING, porter, Traffic Department, Menheniot.

F. PIDDEN, parcel carman, Traffic Department, Dorchester.

J. YEATMAN, wireman Signal Department, Worcester.

C. SHARLAND, carriage cleaner, Locomotive and Carriage Dept., Old Oak Common.

G. SOLMAN, messenger, Goods Department, Cardiff.

O. L. HOUSE, machinist, Signal Department, Reading.

F. SHARPE, shunter, Traffic Department, Portishead.

Figure 25 Railway magazines produced up-to-date memorials of their workers who had paid the ultimate price for their service.

which were under the command of Captain A.S. Littlejohns of the Royal Navy. Although armoured trains had been used by the British Army as early as the Second Boer War, it was the Royal Naval Brigade who did most of the fighting at Antwerp, accompanied by Winston Churchill. As First Lord of the Admiralty, Churchill was in Antwerp to report on the situation. He ordered the British forces there to carry on with their defence of the city. He spent three days on the front line there.

The *Daily Mail* correspondent J.M.N. Jeffries described how he saw an armoured train approach him, stop and fire its naval guns before he was dragged aboard a wooden goods or horse van that was the tail end of what was otherwise a metal train. The train was drawn by two engines and the trucks had been assembled at the Cockerill workshops in Antwerp.

Captain Littlejohns was in overall command of the two armoured trains and in direct command of one of them. The other was commanded by Captain Servais, a Belgian. Jefferies described how all the gunners on both trains were British naval men and that the trains somehow retained a seafaring character. They would stop and fire their guns and move on before the Germans could pinpoint their position and retaliate.

As the Germans approached it was decided that the British and the Belgian forces would evacuate. They marched to Ghent, where the only railway line was still in operation, and boarded five trains. For some reason, about 1,500 men were left behind. Faced with capture, they crossed the border into Holland, and were subsequently interned there for the duration of the war.

The outbreak of war had led to some restrictions for the travelling public. We have already learned that a number of excursions were cancelled in the first few weeks but many of these were restarted quite quickly. The war did not affect the railways in Ireland in the early years but did have some effects later in the war. By November 1914, though, some stations were closed, and as the war progressed, there were more restrictions for the public on the railways.

It was already evident that the French railway system was struggling to provide all that the British Army needed in France as there were problems unloading the supplies at the docks and moving them to where they were needed. The Railway Executive Committee tried to find someone to deal with this problem and settled on Percy Tempest, Chief Engineer of the SE&CR. Tempest is remembered on a plaque on a bridge that he built at

Tunbridge Wells station in 1907. He was helped in his new job by Francis Dent, the company's general manager. It was Dent who was to become a major force in the railway system supporting the troops fighting abroad, but this was to come later in the conflict.

The SE&CR already ran a ferry service between Folkestone and Boulogne and Dent suggested that they take over the running of the port, which was used to supply the BEF. As well as this, they built new buildings and railway sidings to improve the transport system from Boulogne.

There had been some discussion in the years before the war on an idea that would have solved the supply problems to France. The question of a Channel tunnel had been raised in letters to the press. Many had scoffed at the idea but one supporter of it was Sherlock Holmes author Arthur Conan Doyle. Throughout 1913 he had been writing to *The Times*, the *Express* and the *Glasgow Herald* praising the idea. He explained the advantages in the case of war with anyone but France. He said that it would strengthen our offensive and defensive options and prevent

Figure 26 Boat trains, such as the Harwich Boat Train shown here, were common as the railway companies ran them to their ports for the Continental routes that were run on their own vessels. Harwich port was taken over by the Admiralty during the war.

a blockade of shipping by submarine. He obviously had a valid point, despite the criticisms of his idea – one of which was how long building the tunnel would have taken.

It soon became evident how much the railways in Britain had depended on imports for materials when there was a shortage of sleepers in October. There was also a shortage of creosote to treat what sleepers they had. Because it was so easy before the war to import timber, there had been a serious neglect of forestry in Britain and there were calls for help. The aid came from Canada, who sent skilled forestry workers to our aid.

At home, the railways had had a relatively easy time by this point. The first month of the war had been busy getting the BEF to the south coast but even then there had not been too much disruption. This was due to the pre-war competition between so many companies. The majority of large towns had a choice of more than one and sometimes three or four railway services. Because of the crowded system, most pre-war trains had run far from full. This meant that when special trains were called for by the military, there were plenty of spare lines on which the normal services could still run. The system had its drawbacks, however, as when carrying freight, the cars would often return empty to their own company lines. The Railway Executive Committee did much to change this in the following years.

The early months of the war saw a large number of the railway employees volunteering to join the forces. Although some were replaced by women, the number of women taken on was not sufficient to fill all the roles vacated by the men. As well as working on the railway, they were also fulfilling roles in railway workshops, which in the majority of cases had turned to the production of armaments instead of railway equipment.

In November, the Tenth Railway Company RE and two of the special reserve companies followed the Eighth RE Railway Company to France. By this time it was already obvious that the number of RE railway men was totally inadequate for what needed doing. The Director of Railway Transport had already been tasked with creating additional railway construction units. The Railway Executive Committee had begun to recruit men from the British railway workforce for these new companies. A large number of the officers were from British railway companies and many of the others were from overseas railways. Some of the companies were made up of men from the same area or rail companies forming what were, in effect, Pals battalions.

One of these was the 113th Railway Company RE. The origins of the company lie in a meeting that was held at Cheltenham in December 1914. The War Office had granted permission for the raising of a Railway Company of 120 men. This was organised by Lieutenant Colonel William Danvers Waghorn, who had been serving on the North West Railway of India. The company was raised from a list of former members of a volunteer unit, the First Gloucestershire Royal Engineers, which had been disbanded in 1908. Recruitment was organised by the former second in command of the Glosters, Major George Arthur Peake. Enough men enlisted to eventually form a second unit, which became the 114th Railway Company RE. This helped to some extent, but the railway troops were still very short of men.

Although the war was being fought on the Continent, there were fears of an invasion of Britain, so a number of troops were moved to the east

Figure 27 Longmoor was the camp where the Royal Engineers' railway troops were trained during the war.

coast, which was seen to be the most vulnerable spot in the country. Trains were used to transport men to the coastal areas that were thought to be in most danger. It was decided to form a floating force of soldiers based in central England, ready to move at the first sign of a German landing. To be ready to move them at short notice, seventy trains were kept ready on sidings.

Cavalry was still seen as an important part of the army in the war, despite proving to be almost useless against trenches equipped with machine guns. Army units that remained in Britain often employed horses – not just for the cavalry but also to pull horse-drawn vehicles, which were still in widespread use. When they were being transported by train on long runs, information was given out as to which stations had taps and buckets to enable them to water the horses. Some also had multiple taps so that men could fill their water bottles.

To support the anti-invasion force, armoured trains were built. The first was built at Crewe but was a joint project between several companies. It had two gun trucks, two infantry carriages and a locomotive. The gun trucks were 30-ton boiler trolleys from the Caledonian Railway and the infantry carriages were 40-ton coal wagons from the GWR. The engine was a 0-6-2 from the GNR. A month later, a similar one was built.

In November, there was a serious invasion scare when it was thought that the Germans were going to land on the coast of Norfolk, which seemed to justify the concentration on defending the east coast. To combat this, there were plans to run 840 trains carrying troops to the area. This led to some GER lines between Norwich and Cromer being closed to the public for a while.

One of the armoured trains was later kept on the Midland and Great Northern Joint Railway on the Norfolk coast – perhaps due to the invasion scare and events that happened in December when the Germans shelled parts of the east coast from ships. The other was on the North British Railway, north of Edinburgh. The trains were manned by soldiers but the driver and firemen were civilian railway staff.

The War Office had been reluctant to have an armed civilian force guarding the railway, but a volunteer force had been organised that would help in the event of invasion. There was a difficulty with volunteers from the railways in that, if the volunteers were called out and a large number of railwaymen left their duty, then moving the forces to oppose the invasion would be difficult. Eventually it was decided that railway volunteers would operate railway services during a call-out rather than face an invasion force.

Interest in the railway system has been common since the earliest days of the railway. This brought about being able to use members of the public who were railway enthusiasts to help in the war effort in exceptional circumstances. A Mr E.A. Gurney-Smith was a registered motorcyclist despatch rider for the Red Cross in Kent. Due to his amateur knowledge of railways and an ability to speak French, he was also employed as a guide for Belgian refugees. Mr Gurney-Smith claimed that his knowledge of the railway system came from reading the *Railway Magazine*. This detail was published in the magazine along with his story.

His duties involved taking charge of wounded Belgian soldiers and guiding them around the country by train. One of his tasks was to take twenty-three wounded Belgians to Abergavenny. After meeting them at Victoria Underground station, officials allowed the police to reserve a special car on the Inner Circle train to Praed Street. They then boarded a GWR corridor coach with enough room for the men to lie down and ran the train through to Abergavenny.

The following day, Mr Gurney-Smith took nineteen wounded Belgians from Kent to Yorkshire. This involved the use of the SE&CR bogie saloon to Cannon Street, and the Great Northern, which took

Figure 28 Large guns mounted on trains were quite common during the war. The British also used some guns mounted on armoured trains.

them by tank engine to King's Cross and attached them to an express to the north. Mr Gurney-Smith was also responsible for taking recovered Belgian soldiers to Folkestone to return to the front.

The experience of Mr Gurney-Smith wasn't an unusual one. Throughout the war there were numerous volunteer guides employed at London stations. At Paddington, Mr Lort Phillips directed twenty-five guides who would aid members of the forces in boarding the correct train to reach their destinations.

The railway companies were responsible for providing railway hospital trains for service at home and abroad and they also provided hospital facilities on ships. Many of the ships owned by railway companies were commandeered by the navy, and this included ships owned by the GWR. Three of these, the *St David*, *St Andrew* and *St Patrick*, were to become the first hospital ships used in the war.

Despite being taken over by the navy, the adaptations to the ships were carried out by the GWR Marine Department at Fishguard. The ships were fitted with 200 beds, as well as lifts so that the wounded could be comfortably taken to each deck. The ships were already in use in 1914, carrying the wounded back from Rouen to Southampton.

Air raids would come later in the war, but early on there were attacks on the British mainland that had an effect on the railways. On 16 December 1914, Scarborough and Whitby stations were damaged by shellfire from the German ships *Derfflinger* and *Von der Tann*, when four NER

Figure 29 A North Eastern Railway locomotive. The NER was much busier in the war carrying goods from Scotland and the north of England towards London and the south.

railwaymen were killed. Hartlepool station was also damaged when a shell went through the wall at the south end and onto the up platform, damaging a train. In a similar vein, the lines to the south were damaged in a number of places and there was also damage to the dock railways at Hartlepool.

The unopposed ability of the German Navy to attack parts of the country came as a great shock to the population, who had believed in the invincibility of the Royal Navy. Wars in the past had been fought in remote parts of the empire or on the Continent. It was a new experience for the British population to suffer any form of attack and it brought the war home to many of those who experienced them.

Naval bases on the east coast should have been able to offer protection from attacks by the German Navy. One of these bases was at the port of Immingham, which was the base for a number of naval vessels from early in the war. Planning for construction of the port had begun in the early twentieth century as a way of expanding the docks at Grimsby. As owners of the Grimsby docks, the GCR were involved with the development, along with the Humber Commercial Railway and Dock Company.

A new railway line was laid from the GCR line at Ulceby station. Building of the dock began in 1906 and was completed in 1912. The development of the port showed the importance of docks to the railway companies. Three other short railway lines were also extended to the dock – the Humber Commercial Railway to Ulecby, the Barton and Immingham Light Railway from Goxhill, and the Grimsby District Light Railway to Grimsby. The south quay was entirely for coal export, with seven coal hoists that could load 400 tons an hour. This became redundant once the war began as coal exports were suspended.

The Admiralty had been interested in the strategic site of the new dock for some time before the war and a naval oil depot was opened nearby just before the war began. When war broke out, twelve torpedo boats and a number of destroyers from the Seventh Flotilla were based there. More destroyers from the Ninth Flotilla and submarines from the Eighth Submarine Flotilla were added. There was little for the naval men to do in the area and the Grimsby Light Railway was well used by sailors on leave travelling into Grimsby for entertainment.

Just before the end of the year, the commanding officer at Immingham authorised the employment of female clerks because the naval base was

THE WORLD'S MARKETS

. are conveniently reached

— through the —

Great Central Railway

and the

PORT OF IMMINGHAM.

Most Modern Dock Equipment.
Available at any state of the Tide.
All Goods Expeditiously Handled.

Immingham Dock is adjacent to numerous Valuable Sites for New Works and Factories, and in close proximity to Coal and Iron Stone Fields, and the many commercial advantages tend to minimise the cost of :: :: :: production. :: :: ::

Full Particulars of Facilities and Charges can be obtained from the Chief Goods Manager, Great Central Railway, Marylebone Station ; and Information respecting Suitable Sites for Works from the Company's Estate Agent, 12, Paton Street, Piccadilly, Manchester.

SAM FAY, *General Manager.*

Figure 30 When the Great Central Railway built the dock at Immingham before the war, mainly for coal export, they had no idea that it would become an important naval base.

Figure 31 Jersey was an important stage in cross-Channel routes during the war, its railway system being run by the London and South Western Railway.

short of staff. As well as working in clerical positions, women were later employed in the torpedo shed, oiling and cleaning torpedoes. It was a great success and was a first step towards the Admiralty establishing the Woman's Royal Naval Service in 1917.

The docks were to be very important to the war effort and of course many were owned by railway companies. Some of the smaller companies often played a more important role than their size would suggest. The Glasgow and South Western Railway was not one of the biggest but it ran between important industrial centres such as Glasgow and Largs in the north and Carlisle and Stranraer in the south. It was an important link between England and Scotland.

The railway company also had a large number of dock connections, with harbours at Troon and Ayr, and part ownership of those at Stranraer and Girvan. It owned three piers at Renfrew, Largs and Fairlie, and ran steamships on the Firth of Clyde and services to some islands.

Chapter 2

1915

The year 1915 was to be a memorable one for the British railway system. It was to be the worst year for a decade for the number of fatal rail crashes and was also to see the highest number of deaths in a single accident ever to occur on Britain's railways. The year began with an accident: on 1 January, two trains collided on the GER line at Ilford.

According to newspaper reports, a local train had left Gidea Park at 8.20 am for Liverpool Street. It was full of passengers from the Ilford suburbs on their way to London. As it passed through Ilford station it collided with the Clacton to London express on the fast line. The collision cut the Gidea Park train in half at the first class carriage section and both sections were completely wrecked.

The engine of the express went off the line and into a coal yard, and killed a horse. All the fatalities were from the local train and included two GER employees. Some of those who were injured were also GER employees as a number of them lived in the Ilford area and worked at Liverpool Street station. The local train normally followed the Clacton express, which had the right of way, but the signals were for the slow train.

Passengers at the station witnessed the accident and went to help. George Mills, the landlord of the nearby White Horse public house, said that arms were sticking through the wheels of the train and he could see the rest of the bodies. Soldiers, civil guards and police also tried to help. The soldiers were Territorials who had been guarding the line.

One lady was sitting upright but had died of shock. A man who had both legs cut off thanked those trying to rescue him and then died. A list of the ten fatalities was displayed in nearby shop windows for those searching for loved ones. This may seem quite callous now but times were different then.

The accident report, which was written by Lieutenant Colonel von Donop, did not hold back his opinion of the cause of the accident. He

Insure Against

ACCIDENTS

OF ALL KINDS

AND CASUALTIES OF EVERY DESCRIPTION

CLAIMS PAID Exceed

£7,000,000

Write for Prospectus

HEAD OFFICE: 64, CORNHILL, E.C.

Figure 32 Customer insurance was common on early railways, which were dangerous. It seems that there was still a market for it during the war.

claimed that it showed that the normal safeguards, including interlocking signalling instruments, lock and block, and emergency detonator placers, justified themselves. The blame, according to Van Donop, was entirely placed on the driver of the Clacton train. He was the only one who claimed that the signals were not in the danger position.

It was well known that men of military age who were not in uniform were often given white feathers as a sign of cowardice. Many of the men working on the railway were not given the option to enlist as their jobs were too important at home. To show that cowardice was not the reason they were not in uniform, employees were given railway service badges as proof of their vital occupations. Wearing the badges would hopefully stop them from being insulted.

The carrying of troops had not, up until now, made a great deal of difference to the overall running of railway timetables. By the beginning of 1915, cross-London routes were starting to feel the pressure as trains from the north had to pass through London to get to the south of the country. Military traffic on London routes had been heavy from the early days of the war and by this time had increased. The SE&CR had to make cuts to its suburban services and other companies followed their example.

There was an early realisation of the importance of railways to the war effort and the part that Dominion troops could play in it. Canadians were

Figure 33 A South East and Chatham Railway locomotive. Mainly a passenger line, the SE&CR was busy during the war, as were all the companies in the south.

already helping in forestry. The War Office then asked the Canadian government to recruit a force of 500 Canadian men for railway repair and construction work in Europe. The president of the Canadian Pacific Railway, Sir Thomas G. Shaughnessy, was the man chosen to organise the new corps.

Mr C.W.P. Ramsey, the Engineer of Construction of the CPR Eastern Lines Montreal, was granted extended leave of absence and was placed in charge. He was given the rank of lieutenant colonel, and the chief engineer and quartermaster were given the rank of major. There was an A and B company, each commanded by a major who was a superintendent of construction. Each company had 252 men plus officers. One platoon of each company consisted of a locomotive crane crew, blacksmith crew, telegraph crew, timber trestle crew and three labour crews. The other platoon had a track pile driver crew, portable pile driver crew, track-laying machine crew, mixing crew, steam shovel crew, works train crew and two labour crews. Each company also had a dining car crew.

The Canadian Railway force was to play an important part in the construction and maintenance of the railway system on the Western Front. This was often mentioned in the *War Illustrated Magazine*, which

Figure 34 The British were slower than the other countries involved in the war in developing the use of light railways close to the front. When they did begin to use them it was mainly Canadians who built them.

carried photographs of the Canadians at work and explained what an important role they were playing.

Before the outbreak of war, the SE&CR was mainly regarded as a holiday line covering the south coast, although they had already been covering some military bases such as Woolwich and the Arsenal and were now organising other important work. To save the company having to transport so many workers on a regular basis to Woolwich, they built the Well Hall Housing Scheme for workers at the Arsenal. Much of the material for the housing was carried by the SE&CR. Earlier in the war the company had been responsible for moving large numbers of Belgian refugees who had arrived at Felixstowe on fishing boats.

Dover was an established and important port for the military but the government decided they needed more ports, so the Inland Water Transport Department Royal Engineers was formed on the banks of the River Stour, where a new base was built. Construction began around the turn 1914/15 and the base was later extended to become a stores depot for goods to be carried across to France on barges.

The docks were undoubtedly important to the war effort but they were not always recognised as such. When Siegfried Sassoon first joined the army he was sent to Litherland Camp near Liverpool and found that not all his fellow officers were of a high level of competency. There was also of course a great deal of snobbishness involved in military matters at the time. One of his fellow officers became known as 'Pardon Me', and Sassoon described him as one of the most complete failures he had ever come across.

It was interesting to see Sassoon say in his memoirs that this man's social pretensions were unmasked as he was in fact an obscure bank clerk from Liverpool. He was found to be so unreliable that while other officers moved on to the front, he spent two and a half years at the training camp. Despite his incompetence, however, he was placed in command of the guards at the Mersey Docks, which does not seem to have placed much importance on the job.

The docks at Liverpool were regarded as very important. They had a deep sea port facing America and there were 7 miles of them. Unlike other docks in the country, they were not owned by the railway companies but did have strong railway connections. The electric overhead railway

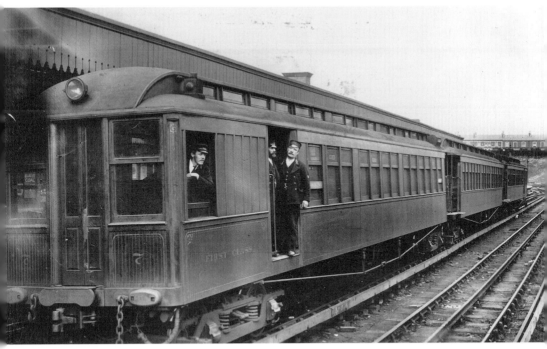

Figure 35 The Mersey Railway was one of the first underground electric railways. It changed from steam after passengers refused to use it, as the steam engines were dirty and unhealthy in the tunnels.

served the docks and was the first of its kind. There were also L&YR steam ships operating from Liverpool to Ireland.

As was the case in the London docks, the men working on the Liverpool docks were employed on a casual basis, so joining the army was an attractive alternative – as borne out by Lord Derby when he was raising his Pals battalions in Liverpool. So many dockers joined up that a shortage of dock workers resulted. To partly combat this, Lord Derby also created a Liverpool Docks Battalion. It was an experiment in running a war industry on military lines and provided a reliable workforce that could be called upon at any time. The battalion was a popular idea with those who supported military discipline for workers. It was not as popular with the unions.

A serious problem developed at Liverpool in the early years of the war. Ships were often queuing to be unloaded – some even waiting a month to be emptied. When they eventually were emptied, often the goods were not put into warehouses. There was also severe congestion on the railways

serving the docks and a shortage of railway cars to carry the goods away
– as well as the 8,000 dockers who had joined the army leaving the docks
very short of men.

When the dockers went on strike, Lord Derby's battalion was regarded
as even more important. The unofficial strike as good as stopped weekend
work on the docks. The battalion consisted of dock labourers who were
all union members and who would concentrate on government work in
the docks but would also be hired out to the Employers' Association in
the Port of Liverpool. Government work at the docks would no longer
be dependent on casual labour. The example of the Docks Battalion
was seen as one that could be used in other industries where the civilian
workforce could not be trusted.

The docks were important to the war effort and one of the more
important locations was Barrow Docks. Alongside the docks were the
ironworks and Vickers Shipbuilding. The Furness Railway, which covered
the area, was very busy working with dock and industrial businesses in
Barrow. The company had managed to fight off takeover attempts by the
Midland Railway, who worked with the Furness to enable them to run a
steamship service to Ireland from Barrow.

Thousands of women were recruited to the armament works at Barrow,
which was short of workers due to a lack of housing in the area. There
had been no great exodus of men from Barrow as the vast majority of
the workers were exempt from military service due to their important
work. The shipyard at Barrow became known as the 'Funk Hole' due to
the exemption of its men. Recruitment rallies were banned in the town.
The workers at Vickers shipyard were supplied with badges similar to
those given to railway workers to show they were doing work of national
importance.

The shell shortage of 1915 was to be a turning point for the railway
workshops. The Railway Executive Committee was asked if railway
workshops could be used to produce more than 2,000 shells a week. These
were to be provided between the GCR, GER, GNR, GWR, L&NWR,
L&YR and NER in their workshops.

A lack of workers was a problem for the railway workshops in the
face of government demands for more shells, even when a number of
machinists were released from the army to help. Many of the workshops
were manufacturing at full capacity but to increase production of shells

HULL AND BARNSLEY RAILWAY.

Australian Liner in the Lock-Pit of the Alexandra Docks, Hull and Barnsley Railway, Hull.

RAILWAY SYSTEM.

Places Hull within easy reach of the Yorkshire, Nottinghamshire and Derbyshire Collieries. These vast coal-fields, annually producing about 70,000,000 tons of coal, are estimated to contain 50,000,000,000 tons.
Connects Hull with the chief British Centres of Commerce and Industry, the great exporting districts with millions of inhabitants requiring food stuffs, raw material, etc.
Express Passenger Trains formed of modern bogie stock, with lavatory accommodation, run between Hull (Cannon Street and Beverley Road) and Sheffield, connecting with the Midland Company's Dining Car and Corridor Fast Trains to the Midlands, the South and West of England, etc.

ALEXANDRA DOCKS, HULL.

Deep Entrance Lock, 85 feet wide, 550 feet long.
53½ acres of Water Space.
210 acres of Storage Ground.
54 Electric and other Cranes.
12 Warehouses.   There are also Sheds, Cellars and Cold Stores.
7 Coal Hoists (each shipping 370 tons per hour).
2 Large Dry Docks.
Regular Steamer Services from and to all parts of the World.

RIVER PIER, HULL.

1,300 feet long.
2 Electric Belt Coal Conveyors (shipping capacity 600 tons per hour each) with anti-breakage and trimming devices.
9 Electric Cranes.
Roomy Warehouse.
Direct Rail Access.
18 feet of water alongside L.W.O.S.T.

For further particulars kindly apply to J. SHAW, Goods Manager, Hull & Barnsley Ry., Hull.
Telegrams:
"JUNCTION, HULL." **EDWARD WATKIN, General Manager, HULL.**

Figure 36 This Hull and Barnsley Railway advertisement seems to place as much emphasis on their docks as on their railway system.

they needed new machines, which were in many cases not those normally used for regular railway production. If there was to be an increase in production then the Railway Executive Committee had to agree to the railway workshops buying the new machines they needed.

This was finally agreed, but only on certain conditions. One of these was that the newly purchased machines would remain government property for the duration of the war. When the conflict finally ended, then the machines could be purchased from the government by the companies involved.

The extra work was to prove difficult to manage and maintenance of railway equipment began to suffer. This situation showed a clear level of antagonism between government departments trying to maintain their own areas of responsibility. The situation led to a later statement by the chairman of the Board of Trade stating that if the railway service was impeded or an accident occurred in consequence of the workshops being engaged in the manufacture of munitions of war then he would hold the Railway Executive Committee responsible.

The situation was partly solved by the increased training and employment of women, who were eventually almost totally responsible for the production of munitions in railway workshops, leaving the experienced railway workers to concentrate on railway maintenance.

There was a great deal of publicity about how the railway companies carried the men of the forces to the war. The experience of soldiers on the railway was not always smooth. Mr John Gibbs was a member of the Stepney Borough Council, the Metropolitan Asylums Board and a transport sergeant in the City of London Rough Riders. He had travelled to Maidenhead on army business to buy a horse with a man named Martin. They returned by train, buying tickets from Maidenhead to Paddington. The men fell asleep on the train and were woken by a ticket inspector at Westbourne Park. Gibbs could not find the tickets but said that he would produce them when the train reached Paddington. The ticket inspector informed another railway official and the doors to the carriage were locked to stop them getting away. This seems quite serious action when dealing with someone on a military task.

When the train arrived at Paddington, there were seven railway officials waiting outside the carriage door. The ticket collector claimed that the men had refused to show tickets or pay their fare and that one of them

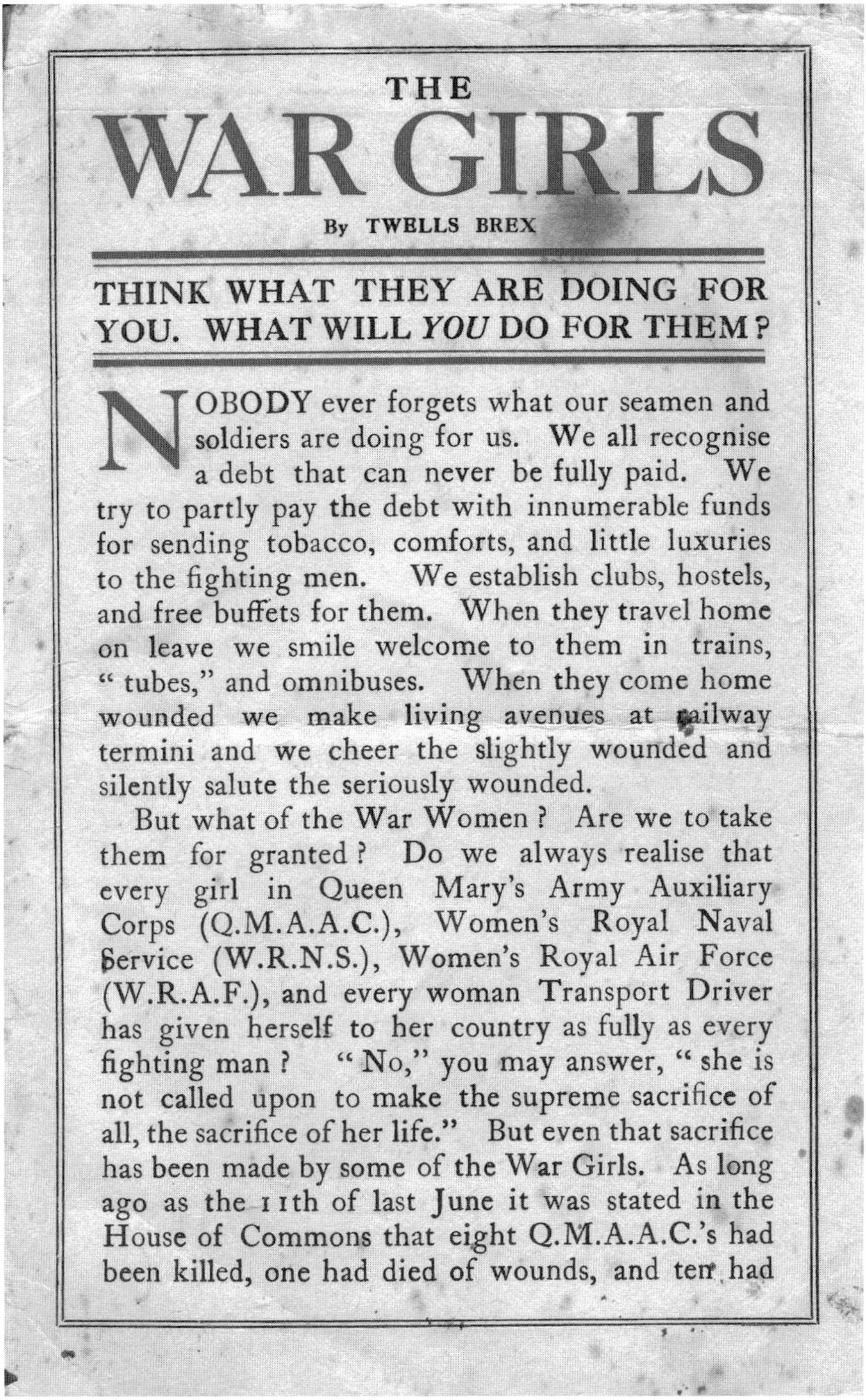

THE
WAR GIRLS
By TWELLS BREX

THINK WHAT THEY ARE DOING FOR YOU. WHAT WILL *YOU* DO FOR THEM?

NOBODY ever forgets what our seamen and soldiers are doing for us. We all recognise a debt that can never be fully paid. We try to partly pay the debt with innumerable funds for sending tobacco, comforts, and little luxuries to the fighting men. We establish clubs, hostels, and free buffets for them. When they travel home on leave we smile welcome to them in trains, " tubes," and omnibuses. When they come home wounded we make living avenues at railway termini and we cheer the slightly wounded and silently salute the seriously wounded.

But what of the War Women? Are we to take them for granted? Do we always realise that every girl in Queen Mary's Army Auxiliary Corps (Q.M.A.A.C.), Women's Royal Naval Service (W.R.N.S.), Women's Royal Air Force (W.R.A.F.), and every woman Transport Driver has given herself to her country as fully as every fighting man? " No," you may answer, " she is not called upon to make the supreme sacrifice of all, the sacrifice of her life." But even that sacrifice has been made by some of the War Girls. As long ago as the 11th of last June it was stated in the House of Commons that eight Q.M.A.A.C.'s had been killed, one had died of wounds, and ten had

Figure 37 A plea to support 'war girls'. It was said that everyone honoured the men serving in the forces but none recognised the war girls who were doing their bit.

had broken the window after the door was locked. One of the officials was a railway policeman who took Gibbs and Martin and locked them in an office. Another man arrived in the office, listened to the story and told the constable to let them go. There appears to have been a level of self-importance in regard to some railway workers who thought that they had a level of power that we would find unusual in railway employees today.

There had always been a number of cheap fares available for passengers on the various railway routes but the Railway Executive Committee decided to end many of these early in 1915 to discourage travelling by the public. However, some cheap fares remained in place to enable visits to army camps by relatives, workers visiting their homes, commercial travellers and a number of club outings.

With Easter approaching, which was normally a busy time, it was decided to cancel more cheap tickets. This was to save fuel and manpower. Again, several clubs and associations managed to avoid the ban. Many excursions were also cancelled but for some reason, special horse racing

Figure 38 Many passenger stations were closed during the war; indeed, Balham does not look busy in this image. An excellent example of station staff in uniform.

trains were still running. There was some criticism of this despite cheap tickets not being available on race trains. The committee defended itself by stating that it was not the duty of the railways to say whether racing should continue but that they were bound to carry passengers who turned up at the stations.

As the war continued, there were more women being employed on the railways in Britain, in addition to those who already had railway jobs before the male employees started to enrol in the forces. The L&SCR seemed to be one of the leading companies in utilising women employees. Early on in the war they established a school for training girls for telegraph work, booking clerk duties and general office work. This was situated at the Signalling School at East Croydon. The school had different classes for each of the occupations being taught.

Often was the case that there was a family tradition of employment on the railways. For example, Miss Strevett, the instructress at the girls' training school, was the daughter of the stationmaster at Hailsham. She had entered the service many years before as a booking clerk at her father's station.

Employment on the railways in Britain was seen as a worthwhile occupation. This was of course true even for those working at the lower grades as employment on the railway was a more secure position than

Figure 39 Training was an important part of railway employment. This image shows the Shrewsbury locomotive department improvement class.

many other occupations of low skill. It was also a desirable position for the better educated members of society. Mr H.E. O'Brian was Assistant Chief Mechanical Engineer of the L&YR. O'Brien had been educated at Eton and the Victoria University Leeds. He had then received his engineering training at Kitson and Company Airedale Foundry, Leeds. Old boys of Eton working on the railways were not something I expected to see. It was, though, very common for those at the top end of railway employment to be very well educated. The standard of O'Brien's education and his position in the company was most likely the reason that he was appointed as a captain and placed in command of the railway troops of 11th Company, Royal Engineers. Ex-public school boys and university graduates were seen as ideal officer material.

At the annual general meeting of the GER, Lord Claud Hamilton MP and Director of the GER said that a unique situation had been created by the war and by the action of the government in regard to the conflict. The prompt assumption of control of the railways had been fully endorsed by the public and had been of invaluable assistance to both the army and the navy. It was not only in transportation that they were helping but also in the manufacture of war goods that private and government factories were unable to turn out quickly enough. As well as providing land transport, the railway companies were giving valuable help to the Admiralty with the various companies' steamships. This was by no means limited to the carrying of troops and stores.

Despite the grave situation regarding the war, Lord Hamilton went on to discuss railway companies' profits, which shareholders were no doubt very keen to know about. The situation had led to speculation as to what dividends the various companies would pay out and there had been some anxiety about this in the previous autumn. This was despite the GER experiencing a more profitable half year up to the previous July than some other companies. This had enabled them to pay the same dividends as they had the previous year.

It was doubtful that this would continue. The GER had launched a new timetable just as war was declared. The staff were depleted by men going to volunteer and the military trains upset the normal passenger timetable. The company would have to face increased prices of all materials necessary to run the railway. There was also a danger of demands for greater wages by the railwaymen, who, Hamilton said, had worked admirably and made

Figure 40 Dover was one of the busiest ports during the war. The Dover Boat Train may have not carried as many holidaymakers during the war but no doubt still carried passengers for other reasons.

many sacrifices for the state. Any wage demands put forward should, he felt, be looked upon favourably as long as they were reasonable.

By this time, increasing costs to the railways could be directly attributed to the war. A number of locomotives had been ordered from German companies shortly before the war began. The reason German companies were used was because their goods were cheaper yet German engineering was of a very high standard. The SE&CR had ordered twenty locomotives from Borsig of Berlin. Ten of these arrived just before the war began. The rest of the order was of course cancelled and was taken over by Beyer Peacock.

Two other companies had also ordered German-built locomotives; the Taff Vale Railway had ordered six from Hanover Engineering and the Port of London Authority had ordered from Hohenzollern of Düsseldorf. Neither of these orders arrived. The Taff Vale order was instead supplied by the North British Locomotive Company. The Port of London order was never completed.

By early 1915, both the French and the Germans had seen the benefits of light railways as a way of providing supplies to the troops. The tracks for these lines could be taken up and relayed quickly without the hard work involved in laying full-size tracks. They provided an ideal form of transport over the often rough ground at the front. The British were slow

FACTORY SITES

¶ The opportunity for business development is now present.

¶ The complex problem of choosing a site which will satisfactorily meet each individual requirement can be solved with a minimum of expense and trouble by taking advantage of the assistance afforded by the organization of the

GREAT NORTHERN RAILWAY COMPANY

¶ There are many desirable sites adjoining the railway and in close proximity to the great coalfields of Yorkshire, Nottinghamshire and Derbyshire.

¶ A copy of "Industrial Progress" (60 pages) giving a wealth of interesting information ; rates, charges for gas, water, electric light and transportation facilities, etc., etc., will be sent gratis on application to Superintendent of the Line, Dept. R.M., 3, York Road, King's Cross, London, N.

Figure 41 Railway companies were eager to promote sites for factories that were on their routes, such as in this advert from the Great Northern. The government were often keen to take them up on their offer for new munitions works.

GLOUCESTER

RAILWAY CARRIAGE AND WAGON COMPANY, LTD.

Manufacturers of all kinds of
Railway Carriages and Wagons for Home, Colonial, and Foreign Governments and Railways

GOODS and COAL WAGONS FOR PURCHASE or HIRE

ALL-STEEL CARRIAGES

PRESSED STEEL UNDERFRAMES AND BOGIES.

ALL-STEEL COACH FOR THE METROPOLITAN DISTRICT RAILWAY

Telegrams:
"SLATER," GLOUCESTER,
"ERCAS," LONDON.

Wheels and Axles and Railway Carriage and Wagon Ironwork

London Office:
VICTORIA STREET,
WESTMINSTER, S.W.

Figure 42 Private companies making railway vehicles were still advertising during the war at a time when many railway companies were unable to make all their own vehicles due to having switched to war work.

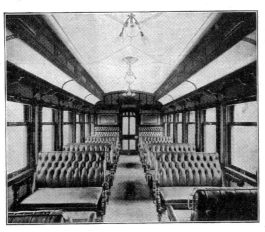

GRAND PRIX, BUENOS AYRES EXHIBITION, 1910.

BIRMINGHAM

Railway Carriage & Wagon Co., Ltd.

MANUFACTURERS OF

SALOON AND OTHER RAILWAY CARRIAGES AND WAGONS OF EVERY DESCRIPTION.

Pressed Steel Underframes, Bodies and Bogies.

Telegraphic Address: "CARRIAGE," SMETHWICK, BIRMINGHAM.
Telephone Nos.:   -   -   .   17 and 107 SMETHWICK.

FOR HOME AND ABROAD.

MAKERS OF HYDRAULIC PRESSED BOSS AND OTHER WHEELS
AND AXLES, IRONWORK, AXLE BOXES, CASTINGS, &c., &c.

**Sole Manufacturers of Dean & Churchward's Eitherside
Brake, and Marillier's Patent Instanter Coupling.**

Works—SMETHWICK, BIRMINGHAM.

Figure 43 Birmingham was one of the leading industrial areas of the country, producing a great deal of war work while still offering to produce railway vehicles.

to accept the idea and were still dependent on motor or even horse-driven transport to supply the trenches. That was until February, when they took over a section of the front from the French and experienced the use of light railways. It wasn't until Sir Eric Geddes took over transport the following year, though, that the British began to make full use of the system.

At home, each railway company had its own challenges. The GCR was carrying a great deal of military transport on its own lines and on its connections with other company lines. It was a joint owner of lines with the Midland and the GNR, connecting Chester, Liverpool, Southport and Manchester among others. It covered a number of industrial towns and had lines to ports on the east coast and to London.

The company carried supplies for overseas and brought back the wounded. There was an example of military and railway co-operation when a new line was laid by the War Department for the huge Clipstone Military camp near Mansfield, but the line was maintained by the GCR. There were other camps built in their area, with new halts opened and new sidings laid to supply them.

The last of the pre-war railway reserve companies was sent to France in February. There were eight construction trains in operation in France by 1915 and each train would eventually have two railway companies, with a captain commanding the train. The trains would carry them to where

Figure 44 Redan Hill in Aldershot was a field fort built by the army in the nineteenth century for training. The railway was built there in 1860 and during the war a large tented camp was sited there.

30th (RAILWAY) LABOUR BATTALION ROYAL ENGINEERS.

WANTED Another 500 MEN
Suitable men in 46 Group may be transferred.
PAY 3s. a day (7 Days to the week)
and the usual Separation and Dependents' Allowances.
ENLISTMENT IS FOR THE DURATION OF THE WAR.
The Battalion will be trained and equipped at Longmoor, Hants, before proceeding overseas.
ALL ORDINARY STANDARDS OF HEIGHT AND CHEST MEASUREMENT WILL BE WAIVED.

Application to be made to
CURZON HALL, BIRMINGHAM.
GOD SAVE THE KING.

Figure 45 An advertisement for men for the 30th (Railway) Labour Battalion. It is interesting that height and chest measurement requirements were waived.

they were needed and the men would set up tented camps while they did their work.

There would often be some preparation of the sites by labour battalions and Chinese labourers were brought in to do much of the heavy work. This was done before the railway companies arrived to construct the railways that were to provide large ammunition dumps and stores depots to supply the men in the front lines.

The war did not put an end to the class system on the railways. Restaurant cars had in some cases been replaced by privately owned Pullman cars to provide meals for travellers. These had previously only been for the use of first class passengers but in what may have looked like a move towards equality, they were now to be used for both first and second class passengers.

It was not quite a wholehearted move to equality, though, as there were plans to provide special separate accommodation for third class passengers. This had been under consideration by the Pullman Car Company Ltd. in conjunction with the LB&SCR and the new cars were under construction. They were of a high standard but not as luxurious as the first class ones. The new carriages were to be run between London and Brighton but whether there would be any expansion to other services would depend on how the use of the railways by the public would develop in the summer months.

Although it appeared that war work was taking precedence over public improvements, this was not completely the case on the Caledonian Railway during the conflict. The stations at Stirling and Carstairs had been almost completely rebuilt. The Aberdeen Joint Station rebuild had been almost completed, as had the stations at Port Glasgow, Carluke and Laurencekirk. There was less chance of bombing in the north and although glass station roofs were removed in some areas due to the danger of being shattered by bombs, Perth General Station had just had a new glass roof fitted.

There had been some restriction on railway excursions by this point. However, Mr H.W. Thornton, General Manager of the GER, said that as terrible as the war was, it was going to be of an advantage to areas with health resorts. This would no doubt lead to an increase in demand for trains to spas and watering places. Perhaps he was thinking of the wounded going to these destinations to recuperate.

A letter to *The Times* in early February complained about soldiers having to hang around on cold stations waiting for trains when they travelled around the country. They frequently found themselves in places at times when everything at the station was closed. The complaint led to action and the SE&CR began to leave a first class waiting room at Victoria station open and heated for members of the forces. It was often filled with sleeping soldiers. Other companies followed suit and a buffet was opened at Liverpool Street station by the GER and a soldier's hostel opened at Paddington.

One reason that the British were late to use the light trench railways in France was that after the Boer War they believed that modern warfare would be fast moving and that trench railways would be of no use as they did not expect there to be a trench war. It was only after experiencing

Figure 46 Birmingham New Street station must have been very busy with the number of industries working in the town and the large number of workers needed.

months of trench warfare that they changed their minds. They settled on the 2-foot gauge, which was the same as the French rails, although they would have preferred the 2-foot 6-inch gauge that they had used in the colonies.

The first engines they utilised were from Leeds but more were needed, so they ordered Baldwins from America. The early ones were 4-6-0s but these were found to be not good enough so they got the better designed 2-6-2s. Eventually they were supplied with locomotives from a number of companies.

There was some doubt at home as to how much progression of trench railways had been made by the British at this time. A letter to *The Times* from a British railwayman in March asked if any of the newspaper's readers could throw light on a question that had been puzzling many British and Canadian railwaymen on the Western Front. He said that we appeared to be using light railway lines in a few areas but not as extensively as the French, while observers reported that the German system for the transportation of troops, wounded men, stores and ammunition was vast and remarkable. In many places behind the British lines, ammunition was still being laboriously transferred to wagons and then to gun positions 100 or 200 yards away. Even the crudest wooden trucks on rails would greatly reduce the labour involved. An expert known to the writer who had had an opportunity to survey the British position put the rate of economy in manpower to be gained by adopting the German plan at a ratio of twenty to one.

The biggest obstacle to the further development of light railways, said the writer, seemed to be the fact that sleepers, rails, coal, locomotives and rolling stock could be ill spared from our home railway system. There was the added problem for the British that all the equipment they needed had to be carried across the English Channel whereas the other countries involved in the war were carrying supplies across land. It soon became evident that motor and horse-drawn transport was not good enough, especially when many roads were in such poor condition.

Figure 47 A Baldwin locomotive, one of the engines used most frequently on the light railways on the Western Front.

The writer went on to ask if, in a few weeks' time, our Canadian kindred could possibly come to the rescue. Light railways propelled by petrol, coal and horse abounded in the Dominion over every variety of terrain. He claimed that hundreds of plants for railway construction with a 2½ to 3-foot gauge were lying idle there owing to the suspension of railway work. The idea put forward by the writer was obviously a view that had already been under discussion amongst those in command.

Other countries had no problems in this area. The French had wide experience of using light railways and their Decauville Company was a leading designer of the method of transport. Decauville was the main provider to the French Army. The French had been using light railways to supply some permanent fortifications since before the war began.

The French found that their Pechot 8-wheeler locomotive was short of power when carrying heavy shells so they also ordered 100 saddle tank locomotives from the Baldwin Locomotive Works in America. They also had some petrol rail tractors. Petrol engines had the advantage of not revealing the train's position to the enemy as the emissions from a steam loco would.

Germany had realised the usefulness of trench railways early in the war, as was mentioned in the correspondent's letter to *The Times*. They had reliable locomotives for narrow gauge rails. Their 8-wheel locos had wheels that could turn to cope with gradients, and they had more than 2,000 of these by the end of the war.

The Germans had been the first to use light railways to supply the trenches. Their systems were in many cases more extensive and efficient than those of the Allies, at least in the early days of the war. It is believed that Arthur Keppel – a German with a small workshop in Berlin – was the first to perfect the portable track. This was a system of steel rails mounted on steel ties and held together with clips, developed mainly for industrial purposes. By 1914, Keppel had a large manufacturing plant specialising in light railways and the German Army had already been using light railways for a number of military uses.

Apart from the first few weeks of the war, the railway companies had not been too badly disrupted and had managed to carry passengers almost as normal. By early 1915, this had begun to change. London was still very congested due to trains from the north crossing over to the south, and this congestion increased as the war continued.

Figure 48 Canadian troops loading light railway trucks to supply the front line. It is interesting to see that despite the move to a more modern form of transport at the front there are still horses in the background.

Most of the companies decided to forgo the use of dining cars and sleepers on many trains so that more passengers could be carried. Football and racing trains were cancelled but each company made its own decisions as to how they would cope with increased government work while still carrying the public. Weekends were also much busier as mines and factories were now staying open seven days a week. The companies were also short of workers as so many men had joined up. Passengers were told they had to carry their own luggage due to lack of porters.

The War Office, although desperate for men in the forces, announced that the Railway Executive Committee were working out a scheme to give increased opportunities for railwaymen to enlist in the army but which did not impair the working of the railway. How this was going to work with shortages of men on the railways was not clear. Until the new scheme was put into operation, recruitment went on as before.

It is common knowledge that during the war many men were criticised when they were not in uniform. Handing out white feathers to those not

unitionslager bei Ham.

Figure 49 A German light railway and a munitions store. The Germans had a very good light railway system from the early days of the war.

serving happened on a number of occasions even though many men were actually unable to volunteer as they were needed at home because of their occupation. As has already been described, this was particularly true of railwaymen and lapel badges were given out by the railway companies so that men could display the fact that they were in war service jobs. Being so small, these badges were not easily seen and there was a move to abolish them and replace them with a khaki armband, which would be recognised as a sign of national service. The scheme was then adopted by the Secretary for War.

There were still a number of attempts to stop the public travelling so as to leave the railway system free for war work. By now, many of the cheap tickets were cancelled and some trains no longer ran. Some stations were even closed, but the public still wanted to travel and often did so despite the warnings not to. This led to more extreme measures. The Great Eastern Railway closed nineteen stations in April as they had insufficient staff to run them. There were complaints from the public so some were reopened. In London, a few stations closed but many of these had competition from bus routes, which were often a cheaper way to travel.

Whilst the GER may have been closing stations, it was expanding in other areas. The railway works at Stratford in London and at Temple Mills covered an area of 130 acres. New buildings had been added before the war, including a modern iron foundry. A paint and carriage shop was now being opened at High Meads as well as a new engine repair shop.

Many large railway stations had by this time provided rooms for service men to obtain refreshments and accommodation for meals,

Figure 50 Large railway terminals began to erect sizeable company memorials after the war but some smaller stations had their own to commemorate the staff at their station who died in the conflict, such as this one at Shenfield in Essex.

which were usually free of charge. These usually depended on how busy the station was with military traffic. In March, the GER opened a large apartment for military use in the centre of Liverpool Street station. On the first day, 400 men used the room and over three days, more than 2,000 men were given free meals. The King visited the room on his way to Harwich and spent some time talking to the men using the facilities.

There was also a hostel opened in Bishopsgate adjoining the station. This was for men who arrived at the station in the afternoon and were waiting for a train due the next day. They would normally have spent the night on the station wherever they could find a space; the lucky ones might find an unoccupied bench. The men could now find a bed and breakfast there for threepence, although any man who had no money was given the bed for nothing.

War memorials were quite rare before the war began apart from a few commemorating those who fought in the Boer War and individual memorials in churches or statues of war leaders. It was unusual then that

Figure 51 One of the first railway memorials was a roll of honour at Paddington for GWR men who had fallen early in the war. After the war, a grander memorial was erected on Platform 1.

the Metropolitan Railway followed the GWR and placed a roll of honour at Baker Street station as early as the beginning of 1915, naming twelve of their staff who had been killed in the war. A permanent memorial was placed there after the war ended. It was what was eventually to become known as the First World War that led to the appearance of memorials in many towns.

The President of the Board of Trade, Walter Runciman, made a speech in the House of Commons in April on the price of the necessities of life. He said that there was no doubt that the rise in the price of household coal, especially in London, was due to the difficulties of getting it there by train. Coal had previously been mainly carried by sea but this was more dangerous due to enemy shipping and German U-boats in the North Sea.

A POUND OF COAL
WILL YER TAKE IT WIV YER GUVNOR ?

Figure 52 Humorous postcards were common during the war, this one a comment on coal shortages.

The coal that did get to London was mainly used by gas and electricity works, large factories and the Underground system. The lack of coal was due to railway facilities being held up by the war as many of their trucks were being utilised for government work. It was also very important, according to Runciman, that the navy should have its coal wherever it wanted it.

Counting his Change.

Figure 52a This postcard shows a woman working in a ticket office, which was one of the roles that women took over after the men had enlisted in the forces.

Because of the measures being taken to reduce the numbers of passengers using the railways in Britain, the GCR sent more engines to France, believing that there would be less need for them at home. There were by this time 40 per cent fewer passenger trains running but passengers were still intent on travelling. The GCR sent eighteen 0-6-0s and fifteen 0-8-0s. They constructed six new locomotives in their workshop at Gorton, along with 2,767 10-ton wagons, 500 low covered wagons and thirty-five brake vans for Egypt. Earlier in the war, they had built two ten-coach ambulance trains and then another in early 1915.

As well as building ambulance trains, railway companies also provided trained ambulance personnel where needed. This was obviously an important activity for railway workers to undertake. In April, the North British Railway held an ambulance challenge cup at the Trades Hall in Glasgow. The tasks included treatment and transport of injured persons. There was also an oral exam. Teams consisted of five men from any of the company stations and twelve teams were involved.

The GCR had fifteen passenger and cargo ships and had owned docks at Grimsby, which were taken over by the Admiralty. The Admiralty also took over the company dock at Immingham. Grimsby became a minesweeping base while Immingham was used by submarines. Three of the GCR's ships had been in Germany when the war broke out and their crews were interned. A large number of the crews of British railway ships spent the war at the internment camp at Ruhleben.

The Admiralty had been quick to take over railway ships and had commandeered more than sixty of them early in the war. There was no obvious thought-out plan for this. The GER had lost so many ships that it could no longer service its Rotterdam route. They then managed to keep it running by borrowing ships from the GCR because their Hamburg route was no longer in service, and yet the Admiralty had not taken the GCR ships that were redundant.

The impounding of railway ships by the Admiralty did not stop at the large numbers they took over early in the war. They seemed to be constantly on the lookout for more ships and the total number they took possession of was more than double the number they seized early in the war. Many of these were lost during the conflict, including some that had still been in railway service.

Figure 53 Many of the bombs dropped on the country were high explosives but there were also incendiaries such as the one shown.

There was an air raid at Blyth, Northumberland, on 14 April, and one of the bombs that dropped near Wallsend, Tyne and Wear, landed near the railway, just missing a train full of passengers on its way to Newcastle on the Tynemouth Line. Newcastle station was closed and an East Coast express was held there during the raid. The lines were soon reopened once the raid was over.

Two days later there was a raid at Lowestoft in Suffolk, when an airship dropped three bombs. Three horses belonging to the GER were killed although most damage was done to housing and a timber yard. In the same raid, six bombs were dropped on Southwold. One of these landed on a railway truck, which caught fire.

There were also bombs dropped on Ipswich and Bury St Edmunds on 16 April. According to one newspaper report, the Zeppelin involved chased a train that was travelling at full speed near Bury St Edmunds and dropped five bombs on it. However, the train reached the station with no damage. The report didn't explain why the airship stopped bombing the train when it reached the station as it would seem to have been an easier target once it stopped.

The fear of bombing naturally had an effect on many of the population. Plaistow in East London was the site of a large railway depot which the Midland Railway had taken over from the London, Tilbury and Southend Railway in 1912. The site had been visited by the Kaiser a few years before the war began. When the conflict started he threatened to bomb Plaistow out of existence. As a result, the local population would

Figure 54 Bomb damage on the bank of the Thames. The bombs in the First World War were not often large enough to damage the tunnels of the Underground in London.

spend each night in the coaling stage there as they believed that it was the only safe place if he tried to carry out his threat.

Air raids were a new form of warfare, with very few examples of such actions before the beginning of the war. The Americans had practised bombing from aircraft in 1910 but it was the Italians who first used bombing in action in 1911 when bombs were dropped on Turkish troops in Libya. Early bombing involved dropping bombs – usually grenades or shells – by hand from early aircraft. It was raids by Zeppelin that moved the method on as airships could carry many more bombs and flew too high to be attacked by aircraft.

The Germans had claimed that there was nothing in international law against bombing British cities. They classed London as a defended city and so its bombing would not constitute a violation of the rules of war. The recognised targets were listed in a report by Karl Henry von Wiegand, a German-born American correspondent, as docks, shipyards, arsenals, barracks and railway stations. No doubt this also included other parts of the railway system such as marshalling yards and any other railway workings.

Southwold had already been bombed. There were a number of very old cannon on Gun Hill, which were hidden during the war as they

Figure 55 British soldiers laying a light railway line near Boesinghe, Belgium, 28 July 1917, during the Battle of Passchendaele (the Third Battle of Ypres). (*George Grantham Bain Collection/Library of Congress*)

could have been seen as making the town a defended one and therefore a recognised target. This was despite it being doubtful if the guns could ever be fired or ammunition that fitted them found.

The raids were reported in the press but government restrictions meant that the actual site of the bombings could not be revealed. Instead, general comments of the damage caused were given and were often very gruesome. One report mentioned how a bomb landed in front of a shop just as a bus was passing and killed nine passengers and the driver, who had both his legs blown off. Bomb damage to busy railway stations would of course be experienced by more people than when bombs fell in isolated streets.

It had become evident by this time that the number of shells needed at the fighting front had been underestimated, leading to a shell crisis despite the increase of production by railway workshops. The Ministry of Munitions was created to deal with this situation. Lloyd George, who was Minister of Munitions from May 1915 to July 1916, wanted men who could deal with problems in production and decided that the best place to look for these was in the private sector.

One of the best run industries in the country was the railways and it was amongst the men running the railway companies that he found his ideal man. Eric Geddes had begun his railway career in America working his way up from humble beginnings as a brakeman on freight trains. In 1904, he joined the NER, and became Deputy General Manager a few years later. Geddes was expected to become General Manager, until the war began, when he was seen as an ideal man to solve the shell shortage at the new ministry.

He was sent to France and found that the transport system was not fit for the job. There was little co-ordination between the separate areas of the system such as the docks, roads and railways. The French railway system had suffered during the war and British aid had not been strong enough to compensate for this. Geddes said that hundreds of British locomotives were needed on the Western Front at a time when there were fewer than fifty already there.

Geddes became Director General of Transportation in France, Director General of Military Railways and also an honorary major general. He even had his own train built to use in France, which was constructed in the NER's York workshop. Geddes began to run the transport system like a railway company. He updated the docks so that the transport of goods ran much more smoothly. His demands on the railway companies did lead to problems at home but the hundreds of locomotives and trucks that he acquired solved the problems of supply in France.

May was to see the worst ever railway disaster to occur during the war when on the 22nd of the month a troop train was involved in a three-train crash at Quintinshill – an isolated spot about 10 miles from Carlisle. The accident illustrated the danger of wooden trains that were lit by gas and *The Times* commented that in eight out of the thirteen accidents in recent years where a fire was involved, it was caused by an escape of gas from the train's lighting system.

Figure 56 The railway workshops were busy during the war but this worker has managed to fit in a break.

The crash at Quintinshill involved an express from Euston to Edinburgh, which was running an hour late. It was made up of two trains that would separate for different destinations. There was also a local Caledonian passenger train as well as the troop train. The accident was caused by two signalmen – George Meakin and James Tinsley. The men had an arrangement whereby the man on night duty would stay a bit later so the day man could delay his arrival. This meant that he could get a lift to work on a local train that passed just after the time he should have been at work.

The first train to arrive was a goods train, which Meakin put on the down loop until the express and the troop train had passed. Then an empty coal train arrived, coming from the fleet at Scapa Flow and was also carrying Tinsley. Meakin planned to put this train on the up loop while he dealt with the local passenger train. Tinsley said to *The Times*

Figure 57 The Quintinshill rail disaster on 22 May 1915 is the worst railway accident in British history and recorded the highest number of deaths, at more than 200.

Figure 58 The accident site was open to passers-by to examine the remains of the disaster.

that as both sidings were full, he put the local train on the up line while the express passed. He said he had no alternative and that it was often done in this way.

It was there fifteen minutes before the troop train hit it. The driver of the local train, David Wallace, leapt from the footplate a second before the impact. He said that the tender of the troop train closed like

Figure 59 The majority of the deaths were among the Territorial soldiers on the train who had volunteered for overseas service and were on their way south.

Figure 60 The troop train involved in the accident was completely destroyed by fire, perhaps due to the gas lighting system. It was believed that carriage doors were locked, stopping the men from getting out.

a concertina and the driver and the fireman were forced into the furnace of their own engine. The wreckage from the collision was then hit by the express from Euston.

The men on the troop train were Territorials who would normally have been only used for home defence, but the 1/7 Royal Scots were being sent abroad as they had volunteered for overseas service. The men were crowded in, eight to a compartment, on a non-corridor train. It was later reported that many of the doors to the compartments may have been locked. This was a common occurrence at the time as many compartment doors were kept locked until trains arrived at their destinations.

There were 500 men on the troop train, including officers on their way south. There were various reports as to the exact number of deaths. The following day's *Observer* said that seventy soldiers had died and 300 were injured. The report stated that the men who had been to the front had seen nothing as terrible as this in the trenches. According to *The Times* the following day, the number of dead was 158. The final death toll was 226. Many of these had been burnt to death.

Among the first witnesses on the scene were Mr and Mrs Dunbar, who acted as caretakers of the blacksmith's shop at Gretna Green where people were married. Mrs Dunbar said that the crash was so tremendous that she thought that the Germans had invaded. The men trapped in the wreckage were calling for help as the fire spread. Some of those who had escaped were forcing open doors. Most of the dead were soldiers but the driver and fireman of the troop train also died as well as some passengers in the sleeping car of the express.

An article in *The Times* published a dying soldier's last words, which were: 'If only it was a fight'. Another description printed in *The Times* described how 'they fought through the wreckage as if storming a German trench'. The dead included 199 soldiers. Tinsley later said that he knew where the local train was but had forgotten all about it.

The Board of Trade report written by Lieutenant Colonel E. Druitt put the blame for the accident squarely on the shoulders of the two signalmen for their neglect of the rules. As well as this, Meakin had still been in the signal box reading a newspaper and telling others about the stories, which distracted them from their duties. Druitt also said that the fire would have spread from the ash from the locomotive even if the train had not been lit by gas. That may have been the case, but surely it would have taken longer to reach along the train than the gas in every compartment.

Although development of the railway system almost stopped during the war there was one improvement on the London Underground: the Bakerloo Line from Paddington was extended to Queen's Park. One of the new stations on the extension was unique as regards its staffing: Maida

Figure 61 Survivors of the Quintinshill disaster. Many of them had helped other survivors out of the carriages.

Vale station was run entirely by women from when it opened in mid-1915 until 1919, when men returned from the war and took over their jobs. Women on the Underground were employed as booking clerks, porters and lift operators.

By the middle of the first complete year of the war, pooling of resources by the railway companies was already a common event. A GER train seen at Stratford in London included wagons from nine different railway companies. These were the GER, GCR, GNR, GWR, L&NWR, NER, Furness, Hull and Barnsley, and North British. It wasn't only wagons being pooled, as was demonstrated when a Midland truck was seen covered with a NBR sheet.

A further unusual event was to see complete trains travelling on other companies' lines. These were normally specials carrying troops or war equipment. This was not always the case, although there was a West Coast train from Edinburgh that went to King's Cross rather than Euston. This was after travelling over NBR, NER and GNR lines. Each company supplied one of their own engines on their own lines for passenger trains. On goods trains, however, engines often worked on other company lines.

Although the pooling and use of other company equipment was to add to the war effort there appears to have been some strange decisions made by the railway companies. One of these was the use of special

ACCEPTING A TRAIN AT HARROW.
L. & N.W. RAILWAY.

Figure 62 The railways in London were busy with trains travelling from north to south. Signal boxes such as this one at Harrow must have been in full-time work.

Figure 63 Many of the lines around London were the first to become electrified. This image shows an early London, Brighton and South Coast Railway electric train.

trains carrying the public to race meetings at Hurst Park. There had already been criticism of running race trains and it led to a statement by Sir Herbert Walker, General Manager of the LSWR and a member of the Railway Executive Committee. Walker claimed that the railways

Figure 64 A North British Railway train. The NBR connected many of the Scottish cities and was in competition with the Caledonian Railway.

did not encourage race going by issuing cheap tickets but were bound to carry any passengers who presented themselves at the station and bought a ticket. The reason for running special trains to race meetings was to avoid crowding on the ordinary service. It was not up to the railways to decide if race meetings should go ahead or not.

The attempts to enrol women into the workforce were in full swing by this time and Lloyd George had a plan to help promote this. He called on the leader of the Woman's Suffrage Movement to help recruit women, not only to the railways but to all industries. Emily Pankhurst organised a rally in July promoting 'women's right to serve'. Lloyd George attended the rally and called on them to do their bit. Thousands of women then came forward to help the war effort.

Men from the Traffic Department and forty drivers and firemen from the Locomotive Department left Euston for New Scotland Yard, where they were sworn in before leaving for Longmoor Camp.

The L&YR had built another ambulance train for use in France and in July it was exhibited at Exchange Station Liverpool. A charge of one shilling was made for the public to enter the train, the money used to buy comforts for the wounded at the auxiliary military hospitals in the city. Almost 5,000 people visited the train, raising £300. This illustrates the interest that the general public had in railway equipment related to the war.

The platforms at the station were decorated with bunting and flags and there were thirty-two members of the St John's Ambulance Association L&YR centre there as well. St John's Ambulance members had attended all the ambulance trains arriving at Aintree since the beginning of the war. It was another way that railway personnel aided the war effort. A number of nurses were also in attendance in the pharmacy and staff cars.

Due to the success of the Liverpool exhibition the L&NWR arranged a similar display at Euston of the more interesting vehicles of one of the hospital trains built at Wolverton Carriage Works. The cars were placed at Platform 12 and the entrance fee was also a shilling. The takings were to provide comforts for the railway troops of the Royal Engineers.

The exhibition was so busy that it was continued the next day. Alongside the general public, the train was also visited by a number of high-ranking officers from the War Office and a number of officials of the other railway companies. Perhaps there was some level of competition

Figure 65 A North British Railway ambulance train – one of many built by several of the railway companies.

where one company wondered if their competitors were doing something that they were not. Also attending were 500 nurses from the London hospitals where many of the returning wounded men ended up, as the trains carrying them often stopped at London terminals. The exhibition raised £325. A few days later, the train was exhibited at Cannon Street station.

In July, a number of men joined a company of a constructional unit of railway troops of the Royal Engineers at Paddington. They were part of a plan to form a company entirely of GWR men. They were the third draft of fifty men. Viscount Churchill, the chairman of the company, expressed his pride in the GWR men who had nobly responded to the country's call for men.

When the GER exhibited one of their ambulance trains at Liverpool Street station in early August, they only charged sixpence entry fee. Perhaps they suspected that the novelty of inspecting hospital trains was wearing off due to the number that had been recently exhibited in London. This train was built at the Stratford Works and was parked at Platform 1. It was later displayed at other stations on the GER system. In total, £1,311 was raised.

Another accident occurred in August when ten people died on an Irish express from Euston to Holyhead on the 14th of the month. The train went off the rails between Stowe Hill Tunnel and Weedon station in Northamptonshire. Seven of the carriages rolled down an embankment. Most of the deaths occurred in the fifth and sixth carriages, which had telescoped.

The cause, according to *The Times*, was the steel rod connecting the wheels of a passing Rugby train, which struck the engine as it passed. The driver of the Holyhead train said that he had seen something fly off the Rugby train as they passed. Another theory was that the broken rod had damaged the line, causing the derailment.

Private James Doherty DCM, who had been on the train, said that he had fought at Ypres and was on his way home to Waterford. His carriage ended up on its side and he had helped others get the injured out while also stopping to help a lady collect £50 in gold that was scattered round her compartment. Another passenger, Joseph Milland of Dublin, had stepped out of the carriage into the corridor to smoke, leaving his 18-year-old daughter in the compartment. The carriage turned over and he later found his daughter dying in a local hospital.

August saw an example of how railway employees who had left to join the forces were still counted as part of the company. A patriotic fete was held in the Wembley grounds of the London and North Western Railway Athletic Club. The company entertained 200 wounded soldiers, many of whom had been company employees and whose places were being kept open for them on their return from military service.

The general manager of the company, Mr Guy Callthrop, and a number of other company officers were present. Music was provided by the Band of the Royal Engineers, Haynes Park Signal Depot. There was catering for 3,000 visitors. Wounds were not a reason for not taking part in events, which enabled all to compete, such as a thread the needle race, blowing up balloons, and darts competitions.

Continuing on from the role that the railways played in the mobilisation of the German Army at the beginning of the war, they were used throughout the conflict to move men to the front and away from it. They also adapted their railway vehicles for other, more recreational, uses. *The War Illustrated* published a photograph of a German bath train in August. The train was stationed close to the front and each carriage compartment

Figure 66 The London, Brighton and South Coast Railway war memorial at Victoria station names all those employees who died during the war.

Figure 67 The South Eastern and Chatham Railway memorial, also at Victoria station, names all their employees who died in the war. The LB&SC and the SE&CR both used Victoria.

was fitted with a bath, which was supplied with hot water from a boiler. Bathing must have been a rare event for the men at the front.

The railways were an important element of the way of life at the time, when for many they were the only form of transport available. In his *Memoirs of a Fox-Hunting Man*, Siegfried Sassoon recalled a discussion with a fellow officer in a dugout at the front. He had been sent a jar of jam with a label showing cherry-growing landscapes. The image would perhaps be thought to inspire memories of the English countryside. However, one of his fellow officers stared at the label and said, 'Do you remember the five-thirty from Paddington? What a dear old train it was.' As he ate the jam, Sassoon said that he mentally passed into a Pullman carriage travelling through Maidenhead. This represents a nostalgic view of train journeys that is perhaps not as prevalent today.

In August, there was an agreement reached with the National Union of Railwaymen whereby employment of women on the railways would not prejudice the re-employment of men after the war. It was also agreed

Figure 68 Female ticket collectors on the London and South Coast Railway. There were claims that ticket fraud increased as women took over the role from men.

that women would work for minimum pay, although the union did try to raise women's pay later in the war. It was obvious that women railway employees were seen as a temporary measure while the conflict lasted.

There was a real need for women to take over some jobs as so many of the railway companies' male employees had volunteered to join the forces. By early in the year, it was evident that many of them had reached the limit of how many men they could afford to lose. Railway employees were now only allowed to enlist if they had special permission to do so.

The GWR were one of the leaders in redirecting staff and working practices to enable more men to be released for military service. To do this they amalgamated a number of cartage establishments, closed down receiving offices from where goods had previously been sent, and replaced the male staff with women workers at offices that stayed open. They also withdrew GWR staff from stations owned by other companies.

There was also a change as to how parcels were sent on the GWR. Waybilling had led to a number of checks being carried out on paperwork connected with parcels being carried on the railway. Previously, a stamp and label system had been in use for local parcels, and this had been adopted for all parcels travelling on any government-controlled railway. This cut down on the amount of paperwork involved.

The railways responded in an ad hoc fashion to air raids early in the war. From early on, there were government instructions to make sure that train windows were covered with blinds. Where there were no blinds in situ, paint or brown paper was used to cover the windows. There was a mixed reaction to raids from the staff. In a raid in the North East in April 1915, all traffic was stopped after a bomb narrowly missed a train and Newcastle Central station was closed. In other areas, traffic carried on during raids.

It wasn't until September 1915 that a subcommittee was formed to decide on a general air raid policy. It was chaired by the general manager of the GER, Sir Henry Worth Thornton, and included members of five of the large railway companies and a Flying Corps officer. The flying officer said that a moving train at night was a useful guide to the enemy, with sparks from the chimney and the open firebox door visible from the air. It was agreed that a raid on a specific area would lead to a shutdown of traffic.

Figure 69 Platelayers at work on the London and North West Railway. At one point during the war, civilian platelayers were recruited to work in France.

It wasn't only the departure of men to the military that was a drain on railway resources. When Ernest Craig MP addressed workers at the Crewe Works on behalf of Lloyd George, Minister of Munitions, he praised the work that men at the works had done on munitions manufacturing. He went on to say that it was also vital to keep up repairs to engines and tenders. This was necessary to keep the railways working that had to deal with the transportation of soldiers.

Lloyd George insisted that repair of railway vehicles was as important as work on munitions but then said that if those involved in railway work could do their utmost, then more men could be released to work on munitions.

The growth of the production of munitions was one of the main reasons for extra work on the railways. This can be seen when looking at the increase in production in individual towns, which was then rolled out across the country. A single factory near Chester was to cause an enormous increase in rail traffic. A factory in Queensferry, 5 miles from Chester, which had previously made boilers, was converted into a government factory to produce gun cotton and TNT explosives. There were between 6,000 and 7,000 workers at the factory, which used up to 300 railway wagons each day.

There was also an enormous army camp 30 miles away from Chester at Kinmel Park, Rhyl, North Wales. There was accommodation for 25,000 men at the camp. A siding from the L&NWR ran into the camp and the need for food and supplies led to an increase in railway staff at Rhyl station.

In Birmingham, much of the normal industrial production was suspended and replaced with government work. One company alone produced nearly 1,000 large tanks, each one over the loading grade of the railways locally and each weighing 30 tons. Another Birmingham firm made nearly 2,000 sea mines. Production such as this was repeated right across the country, leading to the enormous increase in work for the railway companies.

Figure 70 Royal Engineers from the Great Western Railway working in the Dardanelles. Some railway companies had formed their own RE railway units.

The tanks were built by heavy engineering companies, which were based mainly in the midlands or the north. This included the Metropolitan Carriage, Wagon and Finance Company in Birmingham, Brown Brothers in Edinburgh, Armstrong Whitworth in Newcastle, Kitson and Company in Leeds, and the North British Loco Company in Glasgow. Most of these were well known for building railway vehicles and were suited to the production of tanks.

Tanks were the new weapons, which were also top secret and so had to be completely covered so that the public could not see them. The name 'tank' came from them being described as large water tanks to mislead anyone knowing their true purpose. The tanks were hard to transport due to their size and parts had to be taken off so they fitted the loading gauge. There were also very few railway vehicles capable of carrying the tanks. They were mainly loaded onto normal railway trucks, which were not ideal due to the weight of the new weapons. Some companies such as the NER and Caledonian did have a number of special vehicles used for steel works and shipbuilding that were more suitable but these were in short supply.

As well as the general railway workers who were doing their bit in the forces, a number of the top managers of the railway companies were also leaving to join the army. Men who were officers of the railways were becoming officers in the forces, many of them in the Engineer and Railway Staff Corps. Sir William Forbes, General Manager of the LB&SCR, was a lieutenant commandant. Many of the thirty lieutenant colonels and twenty-five majors in the railway units were civilian railway chief officers – some of them still playing a part in running the railways while also holding suitable army ranks.

This was not only the case in the railway forces. When Lloyd George formed the Ministry of Munitions he selected three well-known railway men to be part of this. They included: Mr E.C. Geddes, Deputy General Manager of the NER, who as well as being a lieutenant colonel in the Engineer and Railway Staff Corps also became Deputy Director General of Munitions Supply; Mr Henry Fowler, Chief Mechanical Engineer of the Midland Railway; and Major D. Bain, Carriage and Works Superintendent of the Midland Railway. Major Bain had retired from voluntary service with the Lancashire, Durham County, West Riding of

Yorkshire and Derbyshire regiments in 1907 with the rank of major, so had some military experience.

Mr Geddes was one of a number of railwaymen who had been close to a military career before choosing to work on the railway. He had intended to join the army at the end of the nineteenth century, but instead went to work on the Baltimore and Ohio Railway. He then worked in India before returning to work for the NER.

As well as the British Army building railways in Europe, in South Africa, South African troops were using the railways to take them towards the Germans. The existing railway lines were many miles short of the border with German South West Africa. A new line had to be built from Prieska to Upington on the Orange River, a distance of 142 miles, and then on to Kalkfontein – a further 172 miles. The lines were built in a very short space – at one point, with 5½ miles being built in one day.

In an unusual incident, Sir William Hoy, the General Manager of the Railways for the Union, and General Smuts, Minister of Defence, were arrested by a sentry at Usakos in Namibia, which had just been vacated by the Germans. When told who they were, the sentry said: 'A likely story;

Figure 71 Women working on railway units in a railway company workshop. During the later stages of the war, women had taken over much of the heavy work.

why would two such important men be wandering around in the desert in the night?' They had actually been scouting to see if the Germans were still in occupation of the village.

The London Underground was expanding in 1915, although it was still partly run by different companies. The Bakerloo Line, which was originally the Baker Street and Waterloo Railway, was extended north to Queen's Park, where it met the LMS main line. The line was later extended to Watford but was only running during the week and using the LMS line. The line was by this time a subsidiary to the Underground Electric Railway Company of London, which had been formed in 1902 to electrify the railways making up the London Underground at that time. Just before the war, the first escalators had been built on the Underground at Earl's Court.

The London Underground did perhaps do less for the war effort than many of the other railway companies. It did not, for instance, carry freight or large numbers of troops to embarkation points for action overseas. It

OFF THE BEATEN TRACK

STEPNEY GREEN.

THE VERGE OF THE GHETTO.

Stepney Green, into which the Ghetto has overflowed, is the remains of old Mile End Green, where, long ago, Tyler marshalled the democracy of England for their march upon London. It is a long, narrow garden, which old people remember as common-land, and is enclosed by a medley of mean houses, model dwellings, taverns, synagogues, and Yiddish news-shops, interspersed with a few old mansions, once the homes of sea captains. Against the "Mulberry Tree" is a row of weather-boarded cottages, as neat as any to be found in hedgerow lane. Near by is High Street, with St. Dunstan's, an old country church with tree-shaded churchyard in the heart of the East End. Dean Colet, who founded St. Paul's School, was vicar here for a time. His father, twice Lord Mayor of London, is buried in the chancel, and among others who lie within are Dean Pace, friend of Erasmus and Wolsey's emissary to Rome for the Papal chair; and Sir Thomas Spert, captain of the *Henri Grace de Dieu*, and founder and First Master of the Trinity House. On the wall of the south aisle is a stone of ancient Carthage, set up in 1663. Admiral Leake, who forced the boom at Derry, and was victor in many a stubborn fight at sea, is buried in the churchyard.

STEPNEY GREEN STATION.

For complete series of fourteen walks, write the Advertising Manager, Electric Railway House, Broadway, Westminster, S.W.   BY

Figure 72 An advertisement for the London Underground promoting the history of the East End, interestingly described as on the edge of the 'Ghetto'.

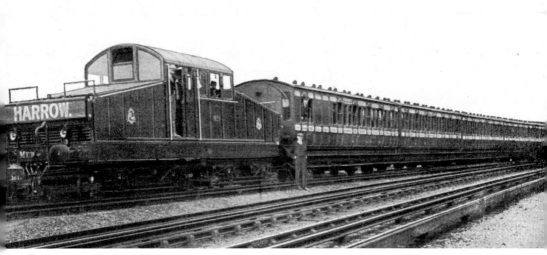

Figure 73 An electric train on the Metropolitan Line. Parts of the London Underground were electrified during the war.

did, however, keep workers in the capital in work and provided a ready-made system of air raid shelters for the public.

The British Army Railway Operating Division (ROD) began work in France in 1915. There were to be 75,000 British railway troops but not all of these were ex-railway employees. A number of men who were deemed unfit for the trenches were sent to the ROD as labourers. They moved supplies to the British front, often using French trains and Belgian locomotives that had been saved from the Germans.

Troops returning from France on leave received a rail ticket to get home once they arrived back in the country. Free refreshments were handed out at Waterloo by volunteers to those on their way home. Large stations such as the London terminals must have seen a large number of men coming and going; whilst some were on their way home, others would be returning to the front.

When Siegfried Sassoon was on his way back to France from Waterloo station he watched how relatives of the men leaving for the front reacted. Commenting in his *Memoirs of an Infantry Officer*, he said that some 'assumed unconcern'; others rushed past him with a 'crucified look'. 'I noticed a well-dressed woman biting her gloved fingers; her eyes stared fixedly; she was returning alone to a silent house on a Sunday afternoon.'

Sassoon mentioned parting at the station again in his *Memoirs of a Fox-Hunting Man.* He asked what those who were watching their son leave for the fighting in France said to each other 'when the train had snorted away and left an empty space in front of them'.

Sassoon's journey from London to Rouen in France took him thirty-three hours, 'a detail which I record for the benefit of those who like slow-motion war-time details' (*Memoirs of an Infantry Officer*). He went on to vent his disapproval of a group of young infantry subalterns who would soon be travelling to the front: 'they'd be crawling up to the war in an over-ventilated reinforcement train, gazing enviously at the Red Cross trains which passed them – going the other way – and disparaging the French landscape, "so different to good old Blighty".' Unlike the troops who travelled in vans designed for horses and cattle, they were 'in clover'; officers travelled in passenger trains even when they reached France.

The increased pressure that some lines were experiencing at home was not always due to the number of military passengers, and not everyone was travelling in discomfort. The Brighton line was carrying a number of first class passengers who would normally have spent the winter on holiday in France or Switzerland but were now heading for England's south coast instead. So great was the demand that a third class service was added in September, using old American cars.

The difficulties faced by the railways had become quite evident early in the war. Lord Muncaster, Chairman of the Furness Railway, said that there had been 220 instructions given by the Railway Executive Committee to the railway companies and this had caused 'enormous and continuous labour and strain'. In early 1915, the Furness Railway had problems supplying the trucks for hauling work from Vickers Works and iron and steel companies on their lines in West Cumberland.

Sir James Bell, Chairman of the Glasgow and South Western Railway, explained how the company, in addition to transporting war goods, had also put their manufacturing establishments at the government's disposal as private firms were unable to turn out military stores and equipment fast enough. This is another example of how railway companies were possibly more efficient than many others. Sir James also went on to mention how companies that owned steamboats were also helping the Admiralty.

Sir Alexander Henderson Bart MP, Chairman of the GCR, explained that the company had carried a quarter of a million soldiers, plus those

G. E. R.

IF YOU ARE DESIROUS OF OBTAINING YOUR SHARE OF THE ENEMY'S TRADE

BUILD AN UP-TO-DATE FACTORY IN EAST ANGLIA.

The Company's Land Agent will facilitate your Enquiries.

ADDRESS :— S. A. PARNWELL,
Liverpool Street Station, London, E.C.

Figure 74 Another advertisement for factory sites, this one for the Great Eastern Railway. It gives an interesting option for obtaining a share of the enemy's trade by opening a factory as many goods that previously came from Germany were in short supply.

on leave, more than 16,000 horses and 1,400 service vehicles. He also mentioned how their manufacturing establishments were at the disposal of the government; this had led to problems in managing repairs of railway works and plant.

Repairs to tracks varied in accordance with need and location. On quiet branch lines it was not necessary to reconstruct the tracks more than once in fifteen to twenty years apart from replacing the odd rail. This was due to light use. On main lines, however, replacement was often needed every twelve to fourteen years, and in very busy areas it could be as often as eight to ten years. Water leakage in tunnels often led to the need to replace track every five or six years. This routine maintenance was obviously difficult during the war due to a shortage of manpower and the necessity to stop trains running while the work was carried out.

To decide when tracks needed relaying, a number of rails in each section were weighed to determine a minimum weight per yard of rail.

The weight and amount of rubbing on the rails was then analysed. Replacement was normally done on a Sunday, when single line working took place while the line was replaced. During the wartime period, about 100 men could relay a mile of track in twelve hours.

The GER had run 2,793 special trains in the first five months of the war, according to Lord Claud Hamilton MP. Their hotel at Harwich had become a military hospital and prices at their hotel at Parkeston had been lowered for naval personnel. The docks at Parkeston, as well as five of the company's steamships, had been handed over to the Admiralty.

There had of course been many railwaymen who had enlisted very early in the war and had been sent into the infantry. As the need for skilled railwaymen grew, many of the early recruits may have regretted their early patriotism as being in the Royal Engineers often offered a safer and more comfortable way of spending the war than that experienced by the infantry stuck in the trenches.

The railway troops did not always have an easier time, though. One of the railway construction companies was even part of the invasion of Gallipoli. This was despite there being no railways for more than 100 miles near the Allied forces and a totally unsuitable terrain for building one.

At Euston, the first complete Railway Operating Corps formed by a railway company were ready to go into camp. They were men of the L&NWR and the corps consisted of three officers and 267 men.

The GER may have been managing to produce war-related items but on the domestic front things were not so advanced. Mr H.W. Thornton, General Manager, was speaking at an open-air concert at the Ilford Hospital Carnival. He admitted that Ilford and other suburban districts of London served by the GER had grown so rapidly in recent years that the company could no longer handle the level of local traffic that was needed. The war had caused a postponement in any definite moves in handling the increase.

There was a different system at work on the railways in Ireland as there was no arrangement between the government and Irish railway companies for the carriage of troops and stores as there was in England. However, the Great Northern Railway of Ireland had displaced its own regular traffic to help the government. The company had also fitted out and equipped an ambulance train comprising nine bogie vehicles, at a cost of £1,300. They were also carrying out government work at Dundalk.

W. J. Phillips (Lieutenant), clerk, Goods Dept. Newport (High Street).

K. J. Chisholm (2nd Lieut.), clerk, Traffic Department, Paddington.

T. L. R. Howells, clerk, Goods Department, Newport (Dock Street).

W. E. Lane, clerk, Traffic Department, Ebbw Vale.

Alfred H. Gentle, clerk, Goods Department, Avonmouth Dock.

L. F. Northcott, porter, Traffic Department, Devonport.

F. Hann, signalman, Traffic Department, Gilfach.

A. Haines, porter, Traffic Department, Hanwell.

J. Rampton, labourer, Locomotive and Carriage Dept, Wormwood Scrubbs.

John Jones, porter, Goods Department, Birkenhead.

W. J. Berrett, policeman, Goods Department, Hockley.

E. Fantham, parcel porter, Traffic Department, Birmingham.

G. F. Hodson, ticket collector, Reading.

W. Bent, carman, Goods Department, Manchester.

F. H. Comley, vanguard, Goods Department, Bristol.

W. Willoughby, office porter, Goods Department, Paddington.

Figure 75 A page full of former employees of the Great Western Railway who died in the war. Published in the *Great Western Railway Magazine*.

By this stage of the war, there had been some attempts to make the railway system run better. The GCR, the GER and the GNR had begun a car pooling scheme, as had the three largest Scottish railway companies.

In October, plans were put in place for how the railways were to react in the event of invasion. As calling up railwaymen who were members of the volunteer force to fight an invasion would have left the railways shorthanded, it was decided they were to carry on with their railway duties instead, which would include moving troops to face an invasion force.

Even before they joined the forces, some railway employees already had skills that would be useful should they be called upon to take part in the defence of the country. Furness Railway had recently opened a rifle club at the Wagon Works at Barrow. There were a number of railway rifle clubs at this time, and shooting competitions were held against other company teams. One of the more interesting ones was in Nottingham, where the Robin Hood Volunteer Regiment wore Lincoln green, but it would be after the war before the Furness Club could compete with the Robin Hoods, who were by this time wearing khaki.

Plans were set in place for what to do in an area of invasion. All trains were to be moved away so as not to be available to the invasion force. Anything that could not be moved was to be destroyed. Lines were to be blocked or destroyed, including those in the docks. Hospitals were to be evacuated as they would be needed for military casualties. The GER area, covering much of the east coast, was thought to be one of the most likely to be invaded and this could prove problematic as much of it was covered with single line working.

There was some debate about evacuating the public in the event of an invasion and it was decided that this would be too difficult as blocking roads with evacuees could hinder troops getting to the area. This was later revised and local police forces were to advise members of the public of evacuation routes they could follow while leaving others open for troop movement.

Due to shortages of railway staff, there were still changes happening in the normal running of the railways. In November, the GNR announced that seats could no longer be reserved for passengers in ordinary compartments or dining cars. Although single seats could not be reserved, on most lines entire compartments could. The 'luggage in advance' system whereby luggage could be sent on to a passenger's destination

Figure 76 The Metropolitan Line war memorial at Baker Street, London. During the war, a large shell that stood next to the memorial was used for fundraising for the troops and is still there today.

before they travelled was also to be cancelled. The situation varied with different companies in regard to the advance luggage service. The dining and sleeping car services of all railway companies, however, were being run on what was described as a minimum basis. The GWR dining car service was now operating with waitresses instead of waiters.

In November there was a Zeppelin raid on a hostelry near Euston station. Three railwaymen employed by the GWR – Foreman Hannon, an ex-soldier, Shipper Tackley and Checker Yarnell – rushed in with buckets of water to put out a fire and rescue some of the people in the station. Their bravery was commended by the company.

The end of the year was to see another fatal accident – on 17 December at St Bede's Junction near South Shields on the NER, where nineteen people died and many were injured. The train involved was the 7.05 am from South Shields, which had seven coaches and was used by businessmen and workmen. It had picked up a large number of passengers from the naval yards at Sunderland's Tyne Dock. The train hit a light engine that was on the same line. The wreckage was then hit by an empty passenger train. The first carriages of the packed train were the worst affected, and they also caught fire. This stopped those who hadn't been injured from freeing those who had. The engine had been assisting a heavy goods train from Tyne Dock and had been standing on the line waiting to return to the dock when it was hit.

One of the passengers, munitions worker John Eales, found himself unable to move in pitch darkness. The compartment filled with gas and one end of it burst into flames. He managed to get out but passengers at the other end of the carriage were screaming. Most of the dead were munitions workers, who *The Times* said had died in their country's service as truly as soldiers at the front. The *Times* reporter went on to say that they had to suffer a more terrible last moment than any soldier at the front.

The GWR Company of Royal Engineers had by this time gone abroad and their send-off from the north of England had been described in *The Railway Magazine* as a boisterous affair as the whole female population of the northern town (which was unnamed in the article so as not to draw the enemy's attention to it) turned out to see them off. During the men's train journeys to their port of embarkation they were provided with refreshments at various GWR stations. The men then boarded a ship to the Dardanelles.

Figure 77 The London and North Western Railway war memorial, which stands in the bus station outside Euston station.

There were some problems in coal production as the year drew to its end. In August, September and October, the output had been greater than the same period the previous year by about 1.5 million tons, but this was still lower than it had been in the same period in 1913. Over the first twelve months of the war there had been a loss of 30 million tons compared with the same period pre-war. During this time there had been 12 per cent fewer men employed underground than there had been before the war, which no doubt was part of the cause.

The war led to an unexpected bonus for trainspotters when unusual engines could be found on lines that they did not normally work on. One keen-eyed spotter was in Glasgow Central station when he saw what he described as a 'query looking locomotive'. The locomotive was painted brown with yellow lines and was a 0-4-4 bunker tank engine. The gentleman inquired about the locomotive with the Caledonian Railway. He was told that the engine was the only one of its class and worked exclusively on the Beith branch of the Glasgow, Barrhead and Kilmarnock joint line. It had recently been at the St Rollox Works for overhaul and was working as a shunter at Central station as a trial. The locomotive was built by Dübs & Co., Glasgow, in 1875.

The French had hoped to organise all railway transport in France during the war but as the end of 1915 approached, they were finding it

Figure 78 Unusual trains were often seen on other lines during the war. This is a London and North Western Railway inspection locomotive and coach.

difficult to manage. They asked the Railway Executive Committee to send 2,000 more wagons. The request was refused as it may have had an adverse effect on the railways at home. The French were not going to take this refusal lightly and were soon to ask again.

Christmas Eve saw a presentation being made at Smithfield when the London District Goods manager of the GWR, Mr H.C. Law, presented Bombardier J.W. Scott DCM with a silver watch. The watch had been paid for by subscription by his former colleagues at Smithfield station. Scott had been in the army before joining the GWR, where he was employed for seven years before returning to the forces when war broke out. He had been awarded the DCM for his gallantry at Hooge in August.

The L&NWR built a batch of ten Prince of Wales class locomotives towards the end of the year and patriotically named them after well-known characters from the war – including those of some of our overseas allies. One of the locos was named after General Joffre, the Chief of the French General Staff. Engines were also named after members of the royal families of our allies, such as the Czar of Russia, the Belgian king and queen, the kings of Serbia and Italy, and the French president, Raymond Poincaré. British names included Sir John French, Admiral Jellicoe and Edith Cavell. Nurse Cavell had recently been shot by the Germans for helping British prisoners to escape from Belgium.

The company later built more Prince of Wales class locomotives and named them after lost ships of the war, including two of their own – the *Albion* and the *Tara*.

Chapter 3

1916

The names on the New Year Honours list of 1916 were to demonstrate how highly regarded were the directors of railway companies. Sir S. Ernest Palmer, who had been appointed a director of the GWR in 1896 and deputy chairman in 1906, was elevated to the baronetage. He was also president of the GWR musical society, a Justice of the Peace in London, a Lieutenant of the City and a trustee of King Edward VII's Hospital for officers, as well as being a member of the council of the Royal College of Music. Another person on the same list was Robert Woodburn Gillan, Knight Commander, President of the Indian Railway Board. Numerous other high-ranking rail officials received honours such as a knighthood.

BRIGHTON RAILWAY MILITARY BAND

Figure 79 Music had always been a recreational pursuit enjoyed by many railwaymen. This is the Brighton Railway military band

In January, the French came back with another request for help with the railway from the British. They asked David Lloyd George, Secretary of State for War, to replace the French railway stock that the British were using in France with rolling stock from Britain. The French had lost a large number of trucks and also some locomotives at the beginning of the war when the Germans advanced quickly and reached them before the French could withdraw.

The British Army's Railway Operating Division had already begun to work in France but were without the use of any British locomotives apart from SE&CR shunting tank engines based at Boulogne. They were also still using some Belgian locomotives that had been saved from the Germans.

At this time, the railway companies in Britain were continuing to play a big part in the war effort and were also doing a great deal for their employees who had either enlisted voluntarily or had been called up when conscription began in 1916. The Newport and South Wales Docks and Railway had lost 144 of their staff, which was just over 14 per cent of the workforce. The men were told that they would be reinstated upon their release from the forces; their military service was still being counted as ordinary service on the railways. The wives and dependants of those serving with the forces were also being paid an allowance by the company.

The Belfast and County Down Railway (BCDR) also kept open the jobs of the 10 per cent of their staff serving in the forces while also paying the men's families five shillings a week. The Caledonian Railway had lost about 2,000 men to the forces but the company had prevented others from enlisting as they were needed to carry out the important work the company had to undertake for the war effort. The Cambrian Railway was in the same situation and the men who were unable to enlist were given service badges by the Railway Executive Committee, showing that they were ineligible for enlistment. This was to be extended to other companies' workers as well.

Although the railway companies all promised to keep jobs open for their employees who were serving in the forces, not all of them offered support to their families. The City and South London Railway carried soldiers and sailors for free and the Dublin and South Eastern Railway had a scheme for supporting enlisted men's dependants, but in 'suitable' cases only.

Figure 80 Many railwaymen who joined the forces did a similar job after enlistment. These are military clerks at Liss in Hampshire, many of whom may well have been railwaymen.

The GER, being one of the larger companies, had lost more men than the smaller companies – about 10 per cent of their workforce, which was 3,600 men. The company had started a GER war relief fund, which was helping the families of their former employees who had died in service. The GWR had lost about 10,000 of their staff to the forces and were also supporting the families of a number of those serving based on the amount of the men's army pay and the government separation allowance. Subsidising so many men's wages must have been an expensive business.

There seemed to have been a very high level of company loyalty even after men had left to join the forces. When G.A. Gibson, assistant engineer on the GCR, joined the 244th Field Company RE he was given the rank of lance corporal. Within two months he was promoted to corporal. After taking courses at Chatham in fieldwork and demolition he was promoted to second lieutenant in command of the 40th Division depot at Doncaster. He was then put in charge of recruiting and after he took this post a number of GCR men also enlisted.

Of course, not every railway employee wanted to serve in the forces and there were a number of reasons for this. Cyril Baker was a clerk for the GWR who lived in Ealing. In March, Baker appealed against having to serve, claiming that he was the only remaining son of a widowed mother, with four single brothers already serving in the forces and one who was married who was waiting to be called up. Baker also claimed to have not recovered from an accident the previous year in which he broke his leg, and he still walked with a stick. Due to this he had been granted a medical extension to not be called up until May. Baker said that he would be unable to march and would be as much service to the GWR as he would in the army.

A statement given in the House of Commons declared that that if they so desired, attested men were entitled to undergo an advance medical examination by the recruitment medical board, the results of which would be taken into account in deciding an appeal. However, it had also been stated that ill health or infirmity was not grounds upon which an application for an appeal may be made. Baker's appeal was therefore judged on his financial situation, not his medical history, as well as his claim to be the only son left at home with his widowed mother. It was determined that Baker lived at home with his mother and a sister. His mother received fifteen shillings and tuppence a week from two unmarried sons serving in the army. The board decided that there would be no financial hardship in Baker joining the army and he had already been granted an extension, so his appeal was denied.

During the war, many of the railway companies had their own hotspots where most of the military work was done. Liverpool was to see the arrival of a number troops from overseas to aid the war effort and the majority of these were dealt with by the L&NWR. The arrival of these troops began slowly, early in the war, with some from Ireland and India, which did not pose too great a problem for the railways. By 1916, the number of arrivals had begun to increase and the increase continued as the war went on, especially after the Americans entered the war.

There were many more Canadian troops arriving in Liverpool by this time, with more than 50,000 of them during 1916. There was also some movement in the opposite direction when the troubles in Ireland broke out in April. Two divisions with transport and artillery were to arrive at Liverpool to cross over to Ireland on the railway ferries.

In spite of many plans for improving and extending the railways being delayed because of the war, the electrification of the L&SWR suburban lines had made some progress. The main power house at Wimbledon and

Figure 81 The Holyhead to Ireland route run by the L&NWR. The image shows the crew on the deck of the SS *Hibernia*.

several substations were near complete. Many of the new electric trains were also ready. The first section to be electrified – Waterloo to Kingston – was almost complete. Lack of progress was not only due to the war but also because of disputes in the building trade and a lack of workers.

There were also delays in train timekeeping. When a train was delayed there was obviously a temptation on the part of the driver to make up the lost time with increased speed, which then increased the risk of accidents. According to *The Railway Magazine*, the most prolific accidents were collisions, and these were for the most part due to unpunctuality. If all trains were on time, they maintained, there would be a suitable interval between each train and less chance of a collision taking place.

One of the main reasons for the late running of trains during the war was adding coaches to a train. This was surprisingly not as common on goods trains on account of braking problems, so maximum loads were stuck to. Passenger trains were different as the coaches had their own braking system, unlike goods coaches, which often relied on the brake van.

The decision to stop traffic during air raids had also led to serious delays. During a raid at the end of January, all traffic in London had stopped for two hours. This saw a crowd of about 4,000 people building up and waiting at Victoria station. One can only imagine the results if a bomb had landed on the station at the time. A little later, a lone plane attacked Dover and Ramsgate, which led to the stoppage of almost all the trains in the south-east and London.

This could obviously not continue so it was then agreed that during a raid trains would continue to run but at 10 miles an hour for goods and 15 miles an hour for passengers. At these speeds there would be no need for firing and so the firebox door could stay closed and not show a light that could be spotted by enemy aircraft. The Defence of the Realm Act of 1914 had also made it law that passengers had to keep window blinds closed when the train was moving, as this advice hadn't always been followed. Passengers often opened the blinds so that they could watch a raid happening despite the danger this brought on themselves and fellow passengers.

The use of electric trains – thought of as the 'trains of the future' – was quite common from early on in the war years. *The Railway Magazine* published details of an article written by 'an ordinary railway journalist predicting how railways would look in 1935–40', in which the unnamed commentator thought that all main line routes could be electrified by

Figure 82 As well as the lines being electrified, so were the signalling systems, as shown in this advertisement.

that time. It was the magazine's view, however, that this was 'too much to expect'.

The railway companies were very keen to keep their workers informed about fellow employees who had gone to war. *The GWR Magazine* was proud to relate that by early 1916, the list of GWR commissioned officers had grown; the names of all of these men were listed in the magazine, including their rank, regiment and previous works department.

The GWR also had its own company of Royal Engineers. The 116th GWR Company RE had been at work in the north of England but were getting ready to go abroad. To increase the size of the company, seventeen more of their men were transferred to the railway troops. Former employees also often maintained links with transport work even when they were not serving with the Royal Engineers. Former employee Lieutenant T.T. Binns, for example, was a member of the Worcestershire Regiment but had been made their transport officer.

This wasn't the case for all railwaymen, even for some of those with great experience in the railways. Mr Wallace F. Young spent seven years in the Locomotive Department of the GCR before taking a position on the Buenos Ayres Great Southern Railway in Argentina. Returning to England when war was declared, he received a commission in the Royal Field Artillery.

The use of narrow gauge railways to supply the men in the trenches was not a new idea. Participants in the war on both sides had been using them but Britain was not as advanced in this as the others. One of the disadvantages of the supply railways was that emissions from steam engines would easily alert the enemy artillery as to where the trains were, making them an easy target. Even though the British were behind in the use of railways in theatres of war, they pioneered the use of petrol-powered four-wheel drive locomotives, known as tractors, to overcome this problem.

The War Office wanted 600mm gauge tractors that were able to pull 10 to 15-ton trains at 5 miles an hour. These were built by a number of companies such as Baguley Cars Ltd., Westinghouse, Hunslet, Baldwin, and Dick, Kerr & Co. These included both petrol and steam locomotives.

The end of January 1916 was to see the sole air attack of the war on the Midland Railway workshop at Derby. The city, which at that time was still a town, had not so far been subjected to any attacks in the war and

Figure 83 The early light railway systems on the Western Front were mainly run by Canadians, shown here carrying shells.

this had led to a relaxation in precautions. Lights were turned on at the workshop and on the 31st of the month, just after midnight, bombs were dropped from a Zeppelin. There were five or six explosions; five people died and £13,000 worth of damage was caused.

The railway workshop at Horwich, near Bolton, belonged to the Lancashire and Yorkshire Railway and during the war was still repairing locomotives despite being very busy on armaments work. They were making 2,000 shells a week where locomotives were normally made and cartridge cases were being repaired in the boiler shop smithy. They were also making 8-inch howitzers.

The L&YR had lines across the north of England. As well as producing guns and shells at Horwich they were doing war work at another of their workshops, at Newton Heath in Greater Manchester. They produced a total of eight ambulance trains – five of them early in the war. Of the first five, two were for the UK and three were for France. The other three were produced later for the Americans when they entered the war. The Newton Heath works also produced a number of different wagons – both general service and water carts, which went overseas.

The company had also owned the largest number of steamships of any of the railway companies. There had been twenty-eight passenger and cargo ships in their fleet. One of their best known routes was from Liverpool to Ireland. The majority of the ships were taken over by the Admiralty and five were lost at sea.

The month of February was to see a major addition to the instruments of war. The development of the tank had been under way for some time as the army tried to decide if the new weapon was to be of any use. It was when the Tank Supply Committee became part of the Ministry of Munitions that the decision was made and the new weapon went into production. The tank had been designed by William Foster & Co. but building them was to be a joint exercise between a number of companies.

One of the companies to build the tanks was the Metropolitan Carriage Works. In 1902 the company had taken over four other firms that were producing railway vehicles. The company built a number of vehicles, including many for the London Underground. During the war it became evident how such manufacturers could adapt their processes. The works were responsible for building almost all of the first 100 Mark 1 tanks. They then went on to build 400 Mark V and 700 improved Mark V tanks. The set-up they had for building railway vehicles was an ideal basis for building tanks.

The work on the tanks was also contracted out to William Beardmore of Glasgow, who were shipbuilders. They also produced numerous types of weapons during the war as well as working on the tanks. After the war they turned their hand to building locomotives. They produced twenty 4-6-0 S69 class and ninety LNWR Prince of Wales class locomotives.

Working in a railway workshop could be a hazardous occupation. The February 1916 edition of the *GWR Magazine* discussed safety in an article that stated: 'despite every conceivable type of warning there were men who persisted in taking needless risks.' The article went on to connect the 'relationship of accidents to the survival of the fittest'.

The article claimed that the taking of risks was due to the harum-scarum nature of some employees, and that this attitude ran in families.

Figure 84 The GWR fire station at their enormous Swindon workshops.

If these family members chose the railways as their calling, they said, then nature would do the rest. The fittest were described as 'those who foresee dangers and greater are his chances of survival'. The idea sparked a lot of interest, as evidenced by the letters that the magazine received in reply. Mr C. Smith of Bedwyn agreed that the theory did appear to be borne out in connection with railway accidents, whilst Mrs Florence Jones of Paddington did not agree at all. She saw that, according to this theory, the safety movement was not only useless but harmful, as checking accidents would lead to the survival of reckless people who would then fill the world with reckless children, who would continue to be a danger.

It would be interesting to discover what basis there was for the ideas put forward in the article. I wonder if the writer believed that his theory would also apply to the men who had joined the forces. Would his harum-scarum types be more likely to be the ones who were injured in the fighting? If this was the case, should these people not be put in dangerous situations?

There was even more danger for the men of the GWR who had joined up. The same edition of the company magazine published a list of twenty-six of their former employees who had lost their lives in service. The site of their death was not listed but their previous occupation on the railway was. One staff member had obviously been more fortunate; Corporal S.W. Lingard, formerly of the staff of the Divisional Superintendent at Bristol, had been awarded the Distinguished Conduct Medal.

The L&NWR had produced four ambulance trains early in the war. A further one had been completed at Wolverton for home service, which was an improvement on the early ones. The train included ten vehicles to carry 120 patients lying down or a larger number who were able to sit up. The beds were capable of providing for patients in both cases. One of the cars had a section that could be screened off for officers. The staff car was fitted with sleeping and dining facilities.

Like others before it, this train was exhibited at a number of stations and a charge of one shilling for entry raised money for the benefit of railway troops. Over £400 was raised in towns including Northampton, Birmingham, Manchester and Leeds.

Figure 85 A Great Central ambulance train showing clear Red Cross emblems.

The danger of invasion on the east coast placed a heavy responsibility on the GER. Their lines covered the area from The Wash to the Thames, which meant that they had to do more in terms of invasion defence than any other company. The problem was that many of their lines were single tracks. As a result, they upgraded junctions with other company lines to allow troops to be moved there more quickly.

The problem facing the GER was mentioned by H.G. Wells in his book *Mr Britling Sees it Through* in 1916. He was discussing why few commuters to London lived in Essex. He said that Essex should be a suburb of London but the problem was Epping Forest and the East End of London. Before a train could carry season ticket holders to London it would have to travel 20 unprofitable miles before reaching the city, and once away from the company's main lines, Essex still lived in the eighteenth century. Difficulty in quickly carrying passengers into London also related to carrying soldiers to the coastal areas.

There were 200 munitions works in the GER area, sixteen shipbuilders and forty-four military camps. Their main workshop was at Stratford in East London, which carried on building railway vehicles during the war. They built 440 wagons to be sent overseas, 225 covered goods wagons, two workshop repair trains for Egypt, and seven ambulance trains – five for France and two for use at home. They later built two more ambulance trains for the Americans. The company sent twenty 20-ton locomotives to France, a 20-ton breakdown crane and twenty brake vans.

The GER were obviously very busy and this led to some attempts at making savings. This was to see the closure of nineteen stations on their lines. A number of London stations were closed such as Bethnal Green and Cambridge Heath. This allowed trains from Liverpool Street to get to their destinations more quickly. The same was done on the Fenchurch Street line, with Shadwell and Leman Street closing. Other stations further afield also closed but the reduction in London stations was expected to be countered by the increased use of trams.

It seems strange that while some stations were being closed, others were opening. A new station was opened at Porthcawl on the GWR, on part of the old dock a quarter of a mile from the old station. The new station was 150 yards from the seafront. The area was popular with visitors and could have up to 10,000 passengers on some days.

The GWR had started an ambulance centre in 1879 and they provided an ambulance man at the movement of all troops in their area, which totalled about 2,000. Their staff also worked with ambulance trains and during air raids, when they were on hand to help. The company gymnasium and rifle range was also used by the 13th Battalion of the Essex Regiment, West Ham, for training.

In France, British railway employees were assisting where needed. The British Army Railway Operating Division was running the Hazebrouck to Ypres line but they had help from former L&NWR employees.

Apart from what was going on in France for the British Army, there was another outbreak of violence in 1916 that was nearer to home. The continuing troubles in Ireland led to the need for troops to be based there and two divisions of men were sent to Riverside, Liverpool, from where they were taken across to Ireland on the L&NWR ships that were still running on the route.

It wasn't only the ships that the Admiralty had taken that were at risk. There was also danger to the ships that the railway companies still owned, as was shown in March when the steamer *Sussex* was torpedoed

Figure 86 New lines being laid by mainly civilian railway workers on captured ground in France.

on the Folkestone to Dieppe route. The ship was sailing under the French flag at the time. There were a number of injuries but the ship didn't sink and was towed to a French port. The *Sussex* was one of the larger vessels that had been used on the joint LB&SC and the West France network. It had also been used on the Newhaven to Dieppe route.

At the time of the attack the ship had been on an ordinary public, non-combatant service, and the passengers and crew were reported to have included a number of persons of neutral nationality. Sir William Forbes, General Manager of the LB&SCR, said that ownership of the *Sussex* had been transferred to the French state railways in January 1914. Such attacks on civilian ships may have had some influence on the events involving the SS *Brussels*, one of the best remembered events involving a railway ship, which occurred a few months after this.

The end of March was to see severe storms hitting parts of the country, especially in the midlands and the north. This also affected other areas as the long-distance expresses from the north were severely delayed in reaching London. Hand-signalling had to be introduced in many areas where signals had been brought down by the storm. Near Port Talbot, a complete signal box was blown down.

Sunderland was to be very unlucky on 1 April. A German airship had left its base to bomb southern or central England but had been blown further north by high winds. The Tyne and Wear area had improved its defences after an attack the previous June. The airship commander therefore decided to attack Sunderland.

Some of the high explosive and incendiary bombs fell on Monkwearmouth station. The bombs destroyed the roof, which reached from the station to part of the goods yard. The roof was never repaired and was later removed. The bombs also fell on the surrounding area and twenty-two people died on the night of the attack.

On 2 May there was an example of how railwaymen often rushed to help even when attacks were not taking place on railway property. Eighteen bombs were dropped on York, including some that landed on a hospital. W.T. Naylor was a bricklayer at York Carriage Works and also a member of the NER fire brigade. He was awarded a medallion by the NER centre of the St John Ambulance association for bravery during a Zeppelin raid when he helped to rescue those injured in the attack.

N.E.R. WAR MEMORIAL,
CITY WALLS, AND STATION HOTEL, YORK.

91885

Figure 87 The North Eastern Railway memorial at York. The city was one of the large railway depots in the north.

Despite efforts to dissuade the public from travelling, they were still doing so in large numbers. The government decided to move the Whitsun holiday in June to August, hoping to put people off making their journeys, but the trains were still busy. Whilst the overall message was that travelling on the railways should be avoided because of shortages of rail staff and lack of resources, conversely there were some additions being made to the railway system. One of these was a new dining room opening at Euston station. The Great Hall was 55 feet long and 37 feet wide. The room was designed in the Renaissance style, the walls oak panelled to a height of 10 feet with railway history illustrations in the panelling. Above the panelling was a tinted frieze and there were arched recesses along the walls. There was also an adjoining smoking room. The design and grandeur of the room suggests that it was provided for better-off travellers and officer class military men rather than the working-class general public, who were more likely to be affected by travel restrictions and lack of resources.

Despite the supposed potential threat of spies and sabotage, there seems to have been few or no restrictions on members of the public watching and recording movement on the railways – an ideal opportunity for those interested in trains. One interested gentleman mentioned that on the Hampstead Junction line at Gospel Oak, used by the L&NWR and North London trains, he had seen 530 foreign engines since the outbreak of the war. These belonged to the L&SWR, Midland, LT&SR, GER, GNR, SE&CR, LB&SCR and GWR. One must wonder how much time this man spent on the station and whether those who were supposed to be guarding the railways were not suspicious of his interest.

Much of the traffic on the railways was carrying goods from north to south. The GNR ran from King's Cross in London almost to York, and then on the North Eastern Line into York and on to Scotland. It carried war supplies from the north to London, where they were passed on to the southern lines. There was a 125 per cent increase in what they were carrying compared to pre-war figures. Of this, 60 per cent was military.

Figure 88 A group of soldiers by a railway line – perhaps guarding it or ready to move by train.

Much of the traffic from the north had to pass through London but the complicated railway system around Kew Bridge and Richmond offered an alternative route. The connecting lines here were owned by a number of companies. Although it was mainly goods trains that used this area during the war, troop trains were also able to use the routes of the North London and the L&NWR lines to bypass the busy London traffic.

The GNR ran passenger trains from Boston in Lincolnshire and had been responsible for carrying large numbers of Belgian refugees from there to Alexandra Palace, where they were gathered before being sent on to other camps. Alexandra Palace later became an internment camp for German and Austrian civilians, from 1915 to 1919, and the GNR used the same route to carry these detainees.

There were a number of accidents on railway lines that serviced army camps. For instance, at the artillery ranges at Shoeburyness in Essex, there were at least three accidents in the middle of 1916 alone. Mr H.E. Johnson

Figure 89 Otto Monsted's margarine factory in Southall, showing how large factories had their own sidings. The building became a military hospital in 1917.

of Cottage Place suffered a fractured shoulder and broken ribs when he was crushed between a train buffer and a wall. Then, Gunner McCartney survived being hit by a train, but it was third time unlucky when Gunner McLoughlin was fatally injured by an engine while wheeling a barrow along a siding when he failed to hear the shout 'clear the line'. Perhaps it was the lack of railway experience of the military personnel that was the problem.

The danger at the artillery site was not only from the military railways. Southend Council had complained to the military that soldiers on their way back to Shoeburyness had been firing their rifles from the train windows. Many years later, a bullet was found in the bedroom wall of one of the rooms at the Shoebury Hotel, which faced the barracks.

The GNR played an important part in Lord Kitchener's last trip in June 1916. He left King's Cross to join HMS *Hampshire* to sail to Russia. Then, half an hour later, a Foreign Office official arrived with important documents that had to go with him. Another special train was sent for this one man and covered the 156 miles to Doncaster in 149 minutes after a four-minute stop at Grantham to change engines. Kitchener waited at York for the documents and later died when the *Hampshire* was torpedoed.

There was an event in June that was clear evidence of German aggression against not only British servicemen but anyone they thought was against them. Captain Charles Fryatt was the captain of the GER Steamship SS *Brussels*, which was still operating on the route between Rotterdam and Harwich.

In March, Fryatt had been captain of the SS *Wrexham*, a GCR ship, and had outrun a German U-boat while crossing to the Continent. Later that same month, U-boat U33 had surfaced and tried to torpedo the SS *Brussels*, of which Fryatt was now captain. He attempted to ram the U33, which had to submerge to escape. In June, when the SS *Brussels* left the Hook of Holland, it was surrounded by five German warships and the captain and crew were taken prisoner. They were sent to the internment camp at Ruhleben, near Berlin, where other captured ships' crews were being held. Then captain Fryatt was put on trial at a court-martial, accused of sinking the U33, even though this was untrue as it had not sunk. He was found guilty and was executed by gunshot.

Naturally, there was outrage at the German actions. The Germans had previously found out that Winston Churchill had ordered that U-boat

Figure 90 The sunken SS *Brussels*, with an inset image of Captain Fryatt, who was shot by the Germans for trying to sink a U-boat.

crews were to be treated as felons. If captured, they should not be treated as prisoners of war but could be shot. The shooting of Captain Fryatt was seen as their response to this.

There was another incident connected to the railways taking place in Africa concerning the armed steamer HMS *Tara*. The *Tara* had previously been the L&NWR's SS *Hibernia* before the war and many of the ninety crewmembers were previous company employees. The ship had been captured and the crew were being held by the Senussi. The Senussi were a religious order based in Libya and Egypt who had been persuaded by the Turks and the Germans to attack British interests in Egypt.

One of the units fighting the Senussi was the Cheshire Yeomanry armoured car section led by Hugh Richard Arthur Grosvenor, the Duke of Westminster. He led an attack on a camp at Bir Asiso and then went on to attack another camp at Bir Hakeim, where the captured crews of the *Tara* and HMS *Moorina* were being held, and he rescued them.

The GNR had lost 10,038 of its staff through their joining the military during the war. This was almost 30 per cent of their total staff. Of these, 980 died. The workers who remained at Doncaster made 18-pounder

Figure 91 There are a number of memorials to Captain Fryatt at Liverpool Street station, Harwich, where he is buried, as well as this one located in Bruge.

guns for merchant ships. Many smaller, previously unarmed ships were given guns to deter attack by U-boats. They also made 13-pounder guns, which were fitted on the backs of lorries, which were then used as mobile anti-aircraft guns.

In early 1916, thirteen members of the staff of the L&SWR had been part of a draft of troops for the Railway Transport Establishment of Overseas Forces. They were sent for training at Longmoor Camp, where the Royal Engineers' railway troops were based. It is interesting to note that the men were employed as office staff when the RE were short of railwaymen.

Some railway employees went on to perform very similar duties in the forces to what they had been doing in civilian life. Sapper A.E. Gage of the 32nd Motor Airline Section RE had been a telegraph lineman in the signal department at Acton for the GWR. He had been awarded the Distinguished Conduct Medal for conspicuous gallantry at Vlamertinge when repairing telephone lines under heavy fire.

There were some railway employees who did a great deal for the war effort without realising it. Francis William Webb had been an engineer designing locomotives for the L&NWR. He died in 1906 but left a large part of his estate to fund the opening of the Webb Orphanage in Crewe. The orphanage was for the children of employees of the L&NWR who were killed in accidents at work. During the war, part of the orphanage buildings became a military hospital.

There were further military connections with Crewe and F.W. Webb. Hewitt Pearson Montague Beames had been educated at Crawley's Military Academy but had entered employment at Crewe and had been a pupil of Webb's. He left to fight in the Boer War in 1900–1901 before returning to Crewe. He became personal assistant to the Chief Mechanical Engineer until 1914, when he joined the army. He then became the commanding officer of the 110th Railway Company RE. Unlike other rail employees who joined the forces for the length of the war, he returned to Crewe in 1916 as Works Manager.

The works at Crewe produced a number of war-related items but perhaps the strangest became known as the Crewe Tractor. It was invented by the chief mechanical engineer at the works, Charles John Bowen Cooke. It was an answer to the problem soldiers at the front had in getting around on the muddy ploughed-up land, which was unsuitable for motor vehicles. The result was a vehicle that was half car and half locomotive. The vehicle was a Model T Ford, which could be driven as a normal car where possible. It could then be converted by removing the wheels to run on the light railway lines supplying the trenches. Over 100 of them were built, although there seems to have been little recorded about their use despite the fact that they must have been an unusual sight.

When the bank holiday arrived in August, which was supposed to be followed by the postponed Whitsun holiday, it was also cancelled to enable factories to carry on working. However, the public still travelled in large numbers despite there being no holiday. The GWR carried more passengers on the cancelled bank holiday weekend than they had on the August bank holiday before the war.

There were more stringent attempts to dissuade the public when fares were raised. Some branch and secondary lines were closed; leave was also cancelled for the military at home to stop them needing to travel.

As well as stations opening and closing there were also wartime adaptations to some. At Queen Street station in Glasgow, on the NBR, a new rest room for soldiers and sailors was opened. The room had been part of the parcels forwarding department. It was opened by Lady Beatty, wife of Admiral Beatty, and was to be run by the Red Cross to provide for members of the forces waiting for trains at the station.

September 1916 saw a serious attack on Nottingham. In spite of there being a blackout, the lights from blast furnaces in the town gave a Zeppelin commander a clear target, although he thought that he was bombing Sheffield. The railway still had to keep working and the lights from the Midland Railway freight station also attracted the Zeppelins, which bombed the town. The freight station was wrecked, as were the tracks and the GCR passenger station.

There were still more engines needed in France; closing some lines at home helped with this as it allowed engines from those lines to be spared for France. The Railway Executive Committee were also discussing taking over privately owned wagons and trying to ensure quicker unloading of wagons to keep them moving, which would have freed more of them up as well.

A new line, station and port were built in Richborough in Kent, although the port was kept secret from the public. Those living in the area must have been well aware of what was going on. Despite this, the new

Figure 92 British trench trains running on lines laid to supply the front lines with ammunition and supplies.

port became known as the Secret Harbour. Large amounts of material were carried on this line. Goods were sent from here across to France, starting with barges and later on with ferries that could carry trains. The harbour itself was camouflaged.

There had already been discussions on what would happen to the railways after the war despite the fact that no one knew how much longer it would go on. In September, Walter Runciman, President of the Board of Trade, asked if there should be an extension of government control of the railways for a period after the war. It was a view that was gaining more support, as was the concept of permanent government control of the railways.

The area around Newhaven, East Sussex, underwent important changes in September when both port and town were designated a Special Military Area. Newhaven had been a very quiet port until it was taken over by the London, Brighton and South Coast Railway in the mid-nineteenth century. They built a line linking it with London, which

Figure 93 Train ferries began to run late in the war and carried complete trains across the Channel. After the war, some of the ferries were used at Harwich.

had a big effect and the port expanded dramatically. They also began to run a ferry service from there to Dieppe in partnership with a French company. The ships they used were commandeered by both the British and the French navies during the war.

The government had given the LB&SCR the task of using Newhaven and later Littlehampton for supply lines to the Continent. Once it became a military area, the station at Newhaven was closed to the public. After this, no one could leave the area without a permit. There was still a lot of traffic, though, as the workers at the port, numbering about 2,500, mainly came from Brighton and Lewes, so had to travel in and out, which must have posed a problem in keeping track of who was coming and going.

Workers' trains were run every day to bring them to the port and old railway carriages were used as a dining area for them. These were laid around a central area which was roofed over and formed part of the dining area. The surrounding carriages provided private dining areas – no doubt for the management.

The LB&SCR were amongst the leaders in electrifying their lines. They had begun with the South London line in the years just before the war, when it was also thought that extending the electrified line to Brighton was practical. As well as the lines making use of electricity, the company telegraph system was one of the busiest sources of Post Office telegrams. They also had a large number of electric signals.

A number of the company's south coast stations also had electric lifts during the war. The Brighton Railway Works was one of the more advanced and was entirely run on electricity by the time the war started. Newhaven Port also had its own power station, although this was mainly used for lighting. The war put a temporary halt to the spread of electrification and it wasn't until after the war that the lines to Brighton became the first main line to be electrified, but this was by Southern Rail after the 1923 grouping into the Big Four.

Newhaven wasn't the only busy point on the company lines. There were still many passengers travelling to Brighton; some were military personnel for the hospitals there, which included one in the Royal Pavilion. The locomotive works in the town was also busy, turning out shells, gun parts and hand grenades. The company's other works at Lancing produced a hospital train along with other railway vehicles.

Workers on the railways had a much higher level of employment benefits than was the case in many other occupations. There was even an insurance edition of the *Great Western Railway Magazine*; as well as receiving their magazine, subscribers also received insurance. This was to prove beneficial to the members of the family of a yard foreman at Newbury, Mr A.E. Stevens. He unfortunately died after suffering injuries in the course of his duties. Mrs Stevens received a cheque for fifteen pounds, which was the thirteenth claim paid by the magazine insurance scheme.

There was by this time a serious shortage of locomotives on Britain's railways as so many had been sent to France. September saw a development in the organisation of finding men to join the forces and to provide enough men for the essential services at home as they were now in short supply. The Manpower Distribution Board would report on the distribution of manpower.

Figure 94 A common scene of damaged railway lines on the Western Front.

By this point, more than 20 per cent of the railway staff had enlisted whilst freight work on the railways had increased by thousands of tons each week. The number of passengers being carried each week had also seen an increase. Carrying out this greater volume of work with fewer workers was presenting a problem. As well as running the trains, the railway companies were also manufacturing war materials in the company workshops so those workers who hadn't enlisted in the military were also occupied on government contracts rather than railway work.

There were still efforts being made to release unskilled men up to the age of twenty-six for military service, despite there already being a shortage of workers on the railways, and there was a grey area between what was seen as skilled and unskilled railway work. Were occupations such as shunters and firemen to be seen as unskilled when they required a considerable amount of training? They were not jobs that new workers could pick up immediately.

This was not the only problem regarding the release of men for military service. The President of the Board of Trade had appointed a committee consisting of Mr H. Courthope-Munroe KC (Chairman), Mr F.W. Goldstone MP, and Mr J.C.A. Ward. Their job was to inquire into cases brought before them. These involved men who had appealed to the general manager of the railway company concerned against enlistment but had still been told to enlist. It was alleged that in some cases the instructions regarding the release of railwaymen for active service issued by the general managers of the railway companies at the request of the Railway Executive Committee had not been followed correctly.

The problem was that it had been claimed that married and skilled men known to be active workers in trade unions had been released for service with the army whilst single, less skilled men had been retained as indispensables. There were suspicions that this was a way of getting rid of union militants. It was also alleged that conscientious objectors who had been recognised by tribunals had been refused further employment by railway companies. Men who were recognised as conscientious objectors were often forced to undertake work of national importance, which working on the railway would seem to be.

Up to this time, the employment of women on the railways had been mainly restricted to using them as ticket collectors and carriage cleaners. There were plans to include women in other occupations such as engine cleaners, porters and even guards. This had to come as the number of men decreased but there was some opposition to allowing women to take what had always been seen as men's jobs. Some of these roles were ones that would have seemed ideal for women, such as clerks. There was, however, another concern. Railway clerks were considered to have

Figure 95 Train drivers were very skilled men. This is Mr J. Lacey at Paddington about to take his train to Cardiff.

middle-class status, albeit lower middle-class. Class was often measured by the nature of a man's employment so when the clerks enlisted, they were often given a commission based on their peacetime occupation. At the beginning of the war, the military were choosy about who got a commission. Even some graduates couldn't get one if they hadn't been to one of the 'better universities'. As the war progressed and the shortage of officers increased, they relaxed their prejudices and widened their recruitment. Those initial class distinctions, therefore, could have been the cause of the general resistance to employing women in high-grade office roles. Before the war, women had worked in railway offices, but usually in more basic administrative roles, which usually involved typing.

There were some unexpected consequences of employing women on the railway system. According to the *Great Western Railway Magazine*, the incidences of ticket fraud had increased along with the number of women employed. This was due to the inexperience of female ticket collectors and having to perform their duties under lamps 'shaded almost to the degree of darkness' due to the blackout. The report claimed that ticket fraud had increased by 100 per cent.

The report went on to say that the chief offenders were women and girls working in munitions. Despite earning good money and already enjoying concessions on rail travel, many travelled with no tickets by telling the ticket collector that they held a season ticket.

It seems that inexperienced ticket collectors were less likely to ask to see the ticket if they believed the traveller had one. One railway company had by this time prosecuted more than 500 fare dodgers. One munitions worker who did not pay a tuppenny fare was fined thirty shillings.

The railwaymen who had enlisted in the forces were not forgotten by their previous employers. Unfortunately, this was often shown in lists of those who had lost their lives being published in company magazines and later commemorated on company war memorials. Before the First World War, memorials had been rare or had commemorated individual persons. After the war, most towns had their own memorial, but railway companies were perhaps one of the

Figure 96 A cartoon of a female ticket collector doing her bit.

only employers to separately commemorate their staff members who lost their lives. There were eventually a large number of memorials to lost staff located at many stations.

Sometimes there was better news, such as the reports on Sergeant Henry Williams of the Coldstream Guards. Previously a stoker in the goods yard at Paddington and an army reservist, he re-joined the forces at the beginning of the war. He was promoted on the battlefield, awarded the Military Medal and was also recommended for the Distinguished Conduct Medal. Private Ernest A. Brewer of the 7th Duke of Cornwall's Light Infantry had been a member of the locomotive department at Southall. His father was a foreman in the goods department at Paddington. He had enlisted in September 1914 at the age of 17. Brewer had already been presented with a medal after saving a boy from drowning while a Boy Scout in 1912. He was recommended for the award of the Military Medal for bravery after he was wounded.

Family connections within the railway companies were common. Regimental Sergeant Major Alfred K. Scott DCM had been a member of the accounts office at Paddington and was the son of Mr J.T. Scott of the Engineering Department at Maidenhead. Scott had been awarded the DCM but was later killed by a shell and was buried on the battlefield.

Figure 97 German POWs being loaded onto trains in France. Prisoners often travelled in greater comfort than the soldiers.

Episodes of bravery were common at the front. When Siegfried Sassoon was awarded the Military Medal, he described the actions that led to it as the sort of thing that people did during a railway accident by trying to save those who were hurt. The railways were playing a part in life in the trenches, as was pointed out by Sassoon in *Memoirs of an Infantry Officer*. While at the front, close to the road to Fricourt, he said that there was a single line railway on the other side of the road. He mentioned to one of his fellow officers that if the war lasted another few years then they would be coming to the trenches every day by train like city men going to the office. In his poem 'Dreamers', written in 1917, he uses the line 'And going to the office in the train', referring to the men in the trenches.

Figure 98 Light railway lines at Amiens.

The light railways were more common in British areas on the front by this time but were still often built by Canadians. They were used for carrying up men and ammunition. They were also used as ambulances to carry the wounded back from the front. Some were horse-drawn open trucks, which resembled a double bed with a man on either side. At busy times a stretcher would be laid across the top of the truck, creating a bunk bed that would accommodate two men.

As well as railway traffic vehicles being in short supply, there was also a serious shortage of wood. When Canadian forestry units were sent to work in Scotland it was the Great North of Scotland Railway (GNSR) that was responsible for much of their transport. The company had been working closely with the Highland Railway from the Aberdeen supply base for the Grand Fleet. They also supplied the minesweeper base at Peterhead.

The company built sidings for the Canadian camps. In addition to the Allied soldiers who were working there, a number of German prisoners of war were also used as labour in the Scottish lumber camps. At this time, German prisoners of war were being used in many areas where workers were in short supply, such as on farms.

Working alongside the Highland Railway was the NBR, which carried large numbers of troops towards the east coast of Scotland in case of invasion. The danger was shown by the presence of two armoured trains based near Edinburgh. The company also had sole access to the naval base at Rosyth.

The NBR showed its importance by being the Secretary Company for Scotland's military command. It had a direct telephone link with the Scottish Command Headquarters. Similar to other railway companies, the NBR lost 4,836 of its 24,625 workforce to the forces.

The first anniversary of the execution of Edith Cavell was commemorated in October. The L&NWR locomotive that had been named after her was at the Rugby workshop for maintenance at the time. The staff decorated the loco with flags and flowers. They also added a sign saying 'Lest we forget'. The engine was parked in a siding in view of the public and a collection was taken for prisoners of war.

The slow increase in British railwaymen working in France was not due to inaction by the government. The French railway companies had wanted to remain in control of their own country's railways and this had been agreed before the war. During the early years of the war there had been enough French railway engineers to keep the trains running. However, it was becoming clear by this time that the war was going to be a long one. The fact that the French were solely running the system was denounced by General Joffre at the end of the year.

The British forces had also made it clear by this stage that they wanted to control sections of the lines, especially in the Pas de Calais area and in Belgium. To do this they began to greatly expand the number of railway troops being recruited from the railway companies at home and abroad.

Meanwhile in France, the British, despite making some progress, were still lagging behind the other powers in the use of light railways. It was Sir Eric Geddes who was to again have influence in revolutionising the British transport system at the front. He requested 1,000 light locomotives and 1,000 miles of track for them to run on. This was only the beginning; once the advantages of the light railways were recognised they began to be used by the British in other theatres of conflict.

As well as being utilised in France, new light railways were being built in the UK to service many of the mines, who were building their own light railways to connect to railway company lines. In October, the East Kent Light Railway built a line for Wingham Colliery. A passenger service began from Shepherdswell to Wingham in October, with a siding to serve the colliery. The EKLR was originally planned before the war as a network connecting nine proposed collieries in the newly discovered Kent coalfields. There was also to be a coal port at Richborough. Most of the pits never managed to reach production.

The fact that there were many light railways operating in the country that were normally used for carrying freight of some kind makes it hard to understand why it took so long for the British to see the advantages of their use in France and other theatres of war. However, the military were never quick to see the advantages of modern developments, as shown by the refusal to promote the use of machine guns early in the war and the failure to accept the tank in its early development.

The war may have increased the cost of living for the public by this point but according to a *Railway News pamphlet*, it wasn't the increased cost of railway transport that had caused it, although this had often been given as the reason. The pamphlet claimed that the increase in the cost

Figure 99 A train damaged in an accident at Little Salkeld, Cumbria, in January 1918 – just one of a number of accidents that occurred during the war.

of transporting food on the railways was negligible compared with the increase in retail prices.

The prices were given for hauling a churn of milk 90 miles and returning the empty; it cost one penny a gallon whilst the retail price of milk was up to two shillings a gallon. Four pounds of high-class fish or 6 pounds of commoner fish carried from Grimsby to London, which is 155 miles, was one penny. Meat from Liverpool to London, which is 200 miles, was a penny for 7 pounds.

The pamphlet went on to explain that producers, middlemen and retailers had all raised their prices in respect of almost every commodity to meet the higher expenses of wartime. However, railway companies had fixed their prices years before when the cost of fuel, materials and labour were out of all comparison to what they were at this time.

There was a more complicated effect on the charges applied by the railways due to the war. This was obviously felt in the rates offices. The staff in this department still had to deal with numerous enquiries as to the cost of carrying a large variety of goods as normal service did continue. However, what had once been regular routes for large goods had changed dramatically.

Before the war, wood for coal mines had mainly arrived at North Eastern and Humber docks from Russia and Norway. The supply of wood from these countries had declined greatly due to the conflict. To ensure that the mines did not go short due to the importance of coal, supplies of wood began to be carried from the Home Counties to the mines, leading to new rates of carrying these items over the new routes.

By this time, there were problems arising on another part of railway property – the canals. Many of the canals in the UK were either owned by railway companies or were leased by them. This led to a two-tier system where workers on railway-owned canals had great advantages over those on private canals.

The railway canal workers were seen as doing work of national importance and were in many cases not allowed to be conscripted into the

Figure 100 The docks at Newport were extended just before the war and there were more than 100 miles of rail sidings, showing the important connection between trains and docks.

forces. They were also entitled to be paid the war bonus. Those employed on private canals could be called up. They were also not entitled to the war bonus, which meant that many of them left to take up more lucrative employment in munitions factories. The result was a shortage of workers on the private canals.

British industries were doing their best to supply the goods needed for the war effort but also recognised an opportunity to expand their businesses by replacing goods that had previously come from Germany. Items such as glass for lighting, and china dolls and other toys, which were no longer available, left an opening for the entrepreneur to fill. One thing missing for British business, however, despite the claims that rail prices hadn't risen by much, were the competitive rates offered by railway companies when they had been trying to outdo their railway competitors. Now that there was a unified system, this no longer happened.

Chapter 4

1917

The new year was to begin as had 1915, with a fatal accident, when on 3 January twelve people died in railway collision near Edinburgh. The 4.18 pm express from Edinburgh to Glasgow hit a light engine on the same line. Similar to the accident in 1915, the train collided with the engine at Ratho station and was busy with workers and soldiers all returning home from the New Year holiday. The first coach telescoped into the second, which was mainly where the worst casualties were.

A witness said that when the crash occurred the lights went out, the doors jammed and the windows broke. In some other accidents there had been rumours of doors being locked. There was no suggestion that this was what had happened here. The servicemen on board had been directed by officers who were on the train and climbed out of windows to help those trapped.

There was a very different situation in regard to the actions of merchant ships by this point in the war. Many of the ex-railway vessels that had been impounded by the Admiralty were by this time armed, along with previously unarmed merchantmen. Mr R.P. Houston MP of the Houston Shipping Company had offered a reward of £2,000 to any British-born master of a British-owned merchant ship for every German submarine that could be proved to have been sunk by their ship.

The arming of merchant ships was an apparent success. According to figures published in the *Railway and Travel Monthly Magazine*, four fifths of attacks on armed ships by German submarines had been beaten off, whilst attacks on unarmed ships had led to the same number of them being sunk.

The war seemed to suit many people who had an adventurous nature. Welsh-born Captain Roger Pocock had an exciting life before he enlisted at the age of 50 at the beginning of the war. He had been a Canadian Mounted Policeman, an explorer and a seaman as well as having pursued numerous other occupations in what he described as a 'wild life'. Part of his experience was in working on the Canadian railways. In early 1916, he became a captain of a company of the Labour Corps in France, during which time he kept a diary of their life at the front. He described the members of his battalion as 'the aged, the disabled, the wreckage of the army and of the nation, some were up to seventy years of age'. They were men 'unfit to fight', although he also mentioned coloured men of the Labour Corps who were young and fit but were not allowed within range of shells. There were some rather strange rules in relation to different races during the war.

The Labour Corps were used to unload trains, build light railways and mend roads. Pocock claimed that his men would watch shells falling with interest without moving, while Chinese labourers had to be withdrawn when under attack because they panicked.

Pocock's men were not the only unusual unit acting as railway workers in France. Sir Eric Geddes asked the Railway Executive Committee early in the year to recruit 3,000 civilian platelayers to work overseas. They were to be chosen from fit men. This was not unusual as it had happened in previous conflicts such as in Egypt in 1882. The railways recruited enough men to form eight companies. Five of the companies consisted of men from Ireland.

The men were contracted to work for three months overseas. They were recruited because the Royal Engineer units were so busy. There were a number of labour battalions such as the one led by Pocock but these did not have the skills needed that experienced railway men could provide.

Although they were civilians, the men were provided with army equipment. Like the military, they often slept in tents or old buildings that were available. They were also fed by the War Department. They often worked nearly twelve hours a day and did at times come close to the front line. The nearest they were allowed to the front was 4½ miles, close enough to be shelled.

Despite the success of the civilian units, at the end of their three-month contracts they were disbanded. The War Office decided not to recruit any more civilian units as they were more expensive than enlisted men, which could cause resentment if they were working with them. It was also a problem that they could not be used close to the front so feeding and billeting them was more difficult. Instead of using civilians,

Officer's Quarters, Longmoor Camp

Figure 101 The officers' quarters at Longmoor Camp, Hampshire. As with most camps, lack of space led to tents being added to increase capacity.

the government decided to obtain additional units for railway work from the colonies.

The loss of staff to the forces had a seriously adverse effect on the L&NWR in January. They were also short of vehicles due to how many they had sent overseas. As a result, they had to close forty-four stations. This saved a number of staff, and trains now did not have to stop at so many stations.

The war had begun to affect the running of all the railways at home by this point. The year was to see some reduced passenger services. This was due to a reduction in available manpower. Some stations also had to close on many other company lines. There was also a coal shortage and by now a large number of locomotives had been sent to France. Fares were increased by 50 per cent but because the Railway Executive Committee was now running the system, ticket inter-availability was introduced, meaning that tickets could be used on different company trains when they were using the same route.

Some trains were increased in size as with more carriages they could take more passengers on a single train. Many of what had been fast express trains were now slower as they stopped at more stations, which also meant that not so many trains were needed on the same route.

The Railway Executive Committee had decided that they would have to do something more extreme to deter the public from travelling. They attempted to do this by making it more difficult to do so. They issued a notice stating that the railway companies of Great Britain would not be able to supplement the scheduled train services during the Easter holiday. Tickets for travel from 4 April to 9 April were only to be available for sale at railway stations, and numbers would be limited to the capacity of the available trains. Previously they had run as many trains as were needed for the tickets purchased.

It didn't seem to occur to the Railway Executive Committee that the British public were much less likely to travel if they had been asked not to than if this had been forced upon them. In their view, the war was being fought for freedom so the public were not going to be ordered around. This was already evident from passengers refusing to close shutters on trains during raids because they wanted to watch.

Something that did have an effect on the numbers who were travelling was the weather, which was very bad during the Easter break. As in times of peace, during the war there was usually an increase in demand for travel during holiday periods. However, the numbers travelling during the 1917 Easter holidays were smaller than they had been in 1913. The trains nevertheless seemed more crowded, but this was because there were fewer of them running, so they were more crowded. Of course the fact that so many men were away in the forces may also have had an effect on families not travelling if the man of the house wasn't there to go with them.

The plans made for the civilian population in the event of invasion varied from area to area. Some areas had plans of what to do if there was an attack but not necessarily an invasion. There had been cases of shelling by German ships in hit-and-run raids. One place that had plans for civilians in the event of an attack was Dover. Being one of the country's most important ports, it was anticipated that an attack was likely. If this took place, the plan was to move the civilians to a point at the back of the town, placing the hills between them and the sea. This would not then involve the use of trains to transport the civilians.

It was believed that any attempted attack by German ships would be seen before they reached the town. There would be radio warnings and a siren sounded, and special constables working in designated areas would then direct citizens to leave their homes. On 21 April, however, German ships managed to evade the watching British naval ships and began a short bombardment of Dover.

As there was no warning there was not enough time to move any of the civilians to the safe area. The German attempts to destroy the town were less than accurate and the shells passed over it, falling on the area where the civilian population would have been moved to if there had been a warning.

To cope with the requirements for larger trains during the war, the locomotives that pulled them also needed to be larger. This was to be a problem for the SE&CR in London. Charing Cross station had been a busy terminus for troops both leaving for Europe and returning home. It was one of the main venues for ambulance trains returning from the front to reach the London hospitals. To reach the station trains had to cross Charing Cross Railway Bridge across the Thames. The down section of the bridge was only being used at half its capacity due to the

Figure 102 Charing Cross station was the departure point for many troop trains headed for France. It was also the terminus for many hospital trains coming back.

weight of locomotives, which had increased since the bridge was built, and they were overloading its capacity. Permission had to be obtained from Parliament to carry out improvements as the work would restrict the access for ships passing under the bridge on the Thames.

The only complaint about the work taking place was from a gas company who ran large collier ships to Wandsworth. The improvements to the bridge would only reduce the clearance in some of the spans from 154 feet to 147 feet and the centre span would not be affected at all. The Port of London Authority was not in opposition to the plan. There were also some calls for Charing Cross station to be closed and replaced with a new station south of the river. The rail bridge would then be turned into a road bridge. It was a plan that would be very expensive and take years to complete and would do little to aid the war effort.

It is always interesting to discover the depth of interest in the railway's workings that some passengers display and it seems that this was no different during the wartime period than it was at any other time. There was an interesting article in the *Railway Magazine* concerning passengers recording the speed of trains. It was claimed that it was possible to determine the speed of a train by timing the quarter, half or whole miles the train had travelled by the number of joints in the rails that the train had passed over. It was thought to require a great deal of practice to manage this method. The timer needed to be familiar with the sounds of the wheels passing over the joints while also knowing the length of the rails.

If that did not sound difficult enough, there were also variations in the sounds made by coaches of different wheel arrangements. All passengers may have been familiar with the rhythmic sound that the wheels make when passing over a joint but few would, according to the article, realise that the noise represented a fixed distance.

In a six-wheel coach the three pairs of wheels can be heard passing over the joint while the average length of the rail is greater than the wheel base of the coach. Every third beat then would indicate a joint. In a bogie vehicle, it is only the wheels on the bogie at the observer's end of the carriage that can be heard passing over the joint. When the explanation went on to explain about eight and twelve-wheel coaches, I began to lose track – especially when rails can vary from 24 to 60 feet in length. It was definitely a method for experts.

In March, the L&NWR named another locomotive after a war hero. The Claughton class 4-6-0 was named *Captain Fryatt*. Fryatt, remember, had become a hero after trying to ram a German U-boat in the GER steamship SS *Brussels* and had been arrested and executed by the Germans.

The use of different company vehicles on other company lines aroused the interest of those with trainspotting tendencies. Often details would be sent to publications such as the *Railway Magazine*. These included details of GER goods engines between Eastleigh and Winchester and LSWR goods engines at Didcot on GWR lines. A reader of the magazine noticed a train at Euston arriving from the north with six brake vans in front, of which five belonged to other companies There were two Highland, two East Coast joint stock and one GNR. There was also an old GWS clerestory roof coach in the middle of the train. The wartime changes had opened a whole new world for trainspotters.

There were sometimes problems with passengers who, because they lived in a democratic country, thought they could do what they liked. The railway companies had to find ways to combat this. It has already been mentioned that blinds had been fitted on trains to stop lights being

Figure 103 Unusual vehicles were often seen on the railways during the war. This is an L&NWR third class picnic car.

visible to aircraft and when a raid began, passengers would often open the blinds to watch. The railways then switched off lights during raids so they would not be seen. Earlier in the war, trains had stopped running during raids but now they could run only more slowly.

There had been some attempts by the Railway Executive Committee to improve the running of the railways. There had been a general carpooling system introduced to stop the movement of empty cars being returned to the owning company. This had involved only open cars at first but now included all cars. This did not of course include privately owned cars, which accounted for about half the car stock on the system. The railway companies owned about 728,700 wagons of all types. Each company had its own standards and built wagons for their own special needs, so some of these had to be excluded from the sharing. Privately owned wagons numbered about 626,200, many of which belonged to mines and quarries.

Another reason that cars were often late returning was because when the cars arrived at their destination they were not unloaded straight away. Many companies saw the cars as a form of warehousing. The railways could charge for delays in unloading but rarely did. There was a move to limit the days that wagons and sheets could be kept after delivery, with more of an emphasis on fines for tardiness. This improved the situation in 1917 but the government and the military didn't do as well and still tended to keep hold of cars far longer than the private companies did.

The NER had a number of special wagons as they served such large shipbuilding and mining areas. Pre-war they had been one of the heaviest coal carriers and were one of the largest dock owners of the railway companies. Much of the coal they carried had once been sent by sea but was now moved by rail because of the U-boat threat. Their area also covered the large military bases at Catterick and Ripon. The company did manage to contribute to the need for railway vehicles overseas by sending fifty locomotives, 4,547 wagons and two steam cranes. They also contributed 27 miles of track.

The NER was one of the leading railway companies in supplying men to the services, although 2,000 of their staff had already been reservists or Territorials. There were 18,339 men from the company who joined up, which was 34 per cent of their workforce. Unlike other companies, the NER actually formed their own battalion. The members of the 17th Service Battalion of the Royal Fusiliers were all men from the company.

It was Eric Campbell Geddes, Assistant General Manager of the NER, who thought that a unit composed of skilled railwaymen of all grades would be of use to the army. He inquired about the idea with the War Office. The Director of Movements told him that the Royal Engineers were able to deal with transport in France, which seemed to be an overestimation, and in response, Geddes formed a battalion of NER men in order to meet the needs.

There were a number of examples of how close the men of the battalion were as well as of their strong connections with the railway that encompassed many family members. A report in the *North Eastern Railway Magazine* explained how Mr A. Wilson, a Permanent Way Inspector, had three brothers – H.A. Wilson, a passenger clerk, W.H. Wilson, also a passenger clerk, and E. Wilson, a goods clerk – all three of whom were members of the battalion.

Some families with several members who were railway workers who had joined up were to suffer terrible loss. J.W. Bentley was a fireman at Gateshead loco works. Four of his sons enlisted – all workers at the same place as their father; Robert and Edward were killed in action.

The battalion became the North East Railway Pioneers. They trained at Hull and then became part of the coastal defence forces in the north-eastern part of the country. Pioneers were used as fighting infantry and also as engineering labour battalions. They later went abroad and became a supplementary force to the Royal Engineers and built light railways to the trenches in a number of the areas that saw the heaviest fighting.

The NER made a number of promises to their men who enlisted. Provision was made for the wives and families of serving men. A married man would have a supplement to the government separation allowance and army pay, which would give the family no less than four fifths of the man's salary at the time he left to join the forces. Special arrangements were also made for single men whose family depended on their wage. Each man's position or an equivalent would be kept open for him on his return and their time in the forces would count as service with the company.

The number of railway companies of the Royal Engineers had grown from two regular companies at the outbreak of war to eventually forty-five companies. They were in operation all over the various areas of conflict. They had been joined by railway companies from other parts of the empire. The tracks and sidings they laid were to provide main line tracks as close to the front as possible for ambulance trains, tanks and all kinds of supplies. The nearer the front they reached, the less distance there was for the light railways to cover.

As well as laying new tracks they were also responsible for repairs to tracks and bridges damaged by artillery fire or bombing from enemy aircraft. The railway lines were often an obvious target for the enemy and many of the men from railway companies suffered fatal wounds. Getting main lines close to the front reduced the workload on horse-drawn and motor vehicles.

The work that the railway companies did for the war effort was often celebrated and the *Great Western Railway Magazine* issued an Art Edition in January, which cost tuppence. With the magazine was an artistic photogravure of a GWR ambulance train built for service overseas. It was described as a souvenir of the GWR's association with the war arrangements.

February saw the introduction of a new and unique service that was to become known as the Jellicoe Specials. Sir John Jellicoe was the admiral

Figure 104 The wagon shop at Swindon. It looks as though an early type of production line was in operation.

commanding the Grand Fleet at the outbreak of the war. The fleet had been moved to Scapa Flow in Scotland and it was important that naval personnel could reach it from the rest of the country. The specials began and became the longest daily service ever in Britain, covering the 717 miles from Euston to Scapa Flow.

The move by the fleet caused a number of problems because of the distance that goods had to be moved. It was a great upheaval for the navy. For many years before the war and in the past, the natural enemies that the navy had to face were Spain and France. Hence, naval facilities were based in the south. Facing enemies that were across the North Sea led to a complete change in naval priorities and bases.

The fleet also needed coal – 600 tons a week – which was carried from South Wales. This was not an easy task for the railway as much of the railway system in the north of Scotland was based on single line working. The new fleet base was perhaps in one of the worst railway service areas in the country. Much of the coal was pulled in trains using borrowed locomotives.

The GWR was responsible for moving coal from the South Wales coalfields. They also covered much of the industrial midlands, the large military bases at Salisbury and ports at Avonmouth, Newport, Cardiff, Barry and Swansea. Once known as the Great Way Round Railway, they used shorter links during the war.

There were a number of munitions works on their lines, including a huge shell factory at Hayes, which needed fourteen work trains a day for their staff alone. The company was also responsible for running more than 1,000 trains for American troops who began to arrive in the country in early 1917.

One of the other places that the Americans landed was at Tilbury in Essex, located on the Thames. The US soldiers were carried away from the port on the London, Tilbury and Southend Railway (LT&SR).

Three of the ambulance trains that the GWR built were shown to the public at Paddington, Birmingham and Bristol. The public were charged for entry and the company raised £2,600, which was given to the Red Cross and the Great Western comfort fund for troops. The Great Western ambulance department also worked with army medical units, the wounded and air raid victims, and there were staff on duty during every air raid, not only those that occurred on railway property.

Although German airships had been used to bomb the country for some time, the first aircraft that dropped bombs was deployed in May. The British anti-aircraft guns were more used to dealing with large airships and had very little chance of hitting the high-flying aircraft, so the ambulance men had more to do.

The GWR produced numerous war supplies at their workshops at Swindon and Slough. They adapted 100 wagons to carry horses and trucks for guns. This was despite losing 32 per cent – 25,479 – of their staff to the forces.

The experience of being employed in a railway works was described by Mr Alfred Williams, who worked at Swindon for over twenty years. Mr Williams was also a writer and was known as the 'Wiltshire poet' as well as writing the book *Life in a Railway Factory*. He described the experience as: 'a yard of about ten acres bounded by workshops and premises built of dingy materials blackened with smoke, dust and steam. From the interior the view is like looking at a fortress, nothing but bricks and mortar, iron and steel, smoke and steam. The sense of confinement within the prisonlike walls renders it dismal.'

Mr Williams was obviously not keen on his workplace but also had a far from high opinion of his workmates, saying, 'The workmen do not think for themselves and if you should be at pains of pointing out anything for their benefit they will tell you that you are mad or will curse you for a socialist. It would need an earthquake to rouse many of the men out of their apathy and indifference.'

Despite Mr Williams's negative comments on the Swindon Works they were obviously very important to the company and to the war effort. In regard to this, the works had their own fire brigade. The works covered an area of 270 acres, of which 50 acres were roofed. The area covered by the fire service also included the passenger station, goods yard and shed.

The brigade consisted of twenty-four firemen, twelve supernumerary firemen and a complementary staff of watchmen. The firemen were also trained in first aid and had to gain a St John Ambulance Association Certificate. The fire station was situated at the London Road entrance to the works. They brigade originally had two manual fire engines to which later was added a steam fire engine, which was then updated to use oil instead of coal. A second, similar engine was employed before the war

Figure 105 Soldiers gathered around an unexploded bomb at Southend, where a number of bombs hit the GER station.

but with the manufacture of more dangerous war-related goods, a Dennis petrol fire engine was added to the brigade's equipment.

There were three companies of construction railway engineers of the Royal Engineers made up entirely of staff from the GWR engineering department. One was in Egypt and two were in France. There were also two civilian companies of GWR engineers in France.

Some of the GWR's steamships that had been commandeered by the Admiralty were being used as hospital or ambulance ships, such as the *Ibex*, which was running to the Channel Islands. The company were also still managing to operate some of their other steamship routes.

Most of the ambulance trains built were of a similar design but this did evolve during the war. The one built by the LB&SCR at the Lancing works was typical. The ward cars were mainly fitted with beds in tiers of three, although some had only two tiers. The beds could also be used as stretchers or altered to form couches for those who could sit. Each ward coach held thirty to thirty-six patients.

Kitchen cars had suitable heating and cooking ranges, with large amounts of hot water available at all times. These cars also contained a mess room and accommodation for kitchen staff. Pharmacy cars had a treatment room, an operating table and an office for the doctor. There would also be a staff car for the doctors and nurses, with living accommodation. The LB&SCR train had seven bogie coaches, two kitchen cars, a pharmacy car and four wards.

The appeal system against being called up was in action again in April, when Harry Holland, a dock wharf and railway carman of Gunnersbury appealed against being called up. Holland had already appealed in June 1916 against serving and was supported by his employer. It turned out that although described as a railway carman, he was actually employed by his father, a market trader at Brentford Market, and his occupation involved taking stock from the railway to the market. Following his previous appeal he was told he would not be called up until April 1917. As a result, a solicitor applied for a new appeal as he was described as being in a certified occupation, plus his wife had been taken ill and was subject to regular hospital admittances. His appeal was refused.

The German Army used the railway system to move their troops into position at the outset of the war but according to German soldier and author Ernst Jünger, they continued to use it throughout the war. Jünger, in his memoir *Storm of Steel,* comments on being moved by train on a number of occasions from one area of conflict to another. He also explained that the sound of trains was not always welcome: 'The habit of jumping was common at any sound whether it was a train clattering past or a book falling to the floor.'

Jünger also describes an attack on a train at Épehy when he was returning from hospital to his unit after a wound. 'There was a series of explosions, the twisted wreckage of freight wagons showed that the attack was in earnest.' He went on to explain how he and other occupants jumped out of the train and took cover behind the embankment. Bleeding horses were led out of a cattle truck but it seemed that they were the only casualties.

Despite the Germans making full use of the railways themselves when they began to pull back to the Hindenburg Line in early 1917, they made sure that the railway lines they left behind were of no use to the advancing Allies. They destroyed as much of the tracks as they could and even some of the stations, such as the one at Roye, in the department of the Somme. This was described in the *War Budget Magazine* as an 'act of wanton outrage'.

There was an ambitious plan to reduce the large losses incurred in early battles when large tunnels were dug at Arras where troops could hide and then come out and attack the Germans by surprise. The Boves were underground caves and tunnel networks created by quarrying that were already in existence. They were extended by New Zealand tunnellers and ran from the centre of Arras to the German lines. There was room for 25,000 men in the tunnels, which were fitted with electricity, running water, kitchens, toilets and even an underground railway system.

When Siegfried Sassoon was wounded he had experience of being carried in a hospital train. The train carried him along with thirty-four other officers and 500 men. He described the passengers as those who had escaped from the horrors of the war which were still visualised in their minds. Many were still wearing boots and clothes caked with mud from the trenches. Some of the men were dying: 'Dying for their country in comparative comfort.'

In May, Sassoon found himself in a railway terminus hotel that had been commandeered for the convalescent officers. The Hotel Great Central was built by the GCR. It was next to their terminus at Paddington. Despite being at one of the smaller London termini, the hotel was one of London's grandest railway hotels. It had a clock tower and was built around a central courtyard.

Sassoon was not happy there. He described it as more military than therapeutic. The commandant was a non-combatant brigadier general who was not popular with the convalescents due to his methods. Despite many of the inhabitants waiting to be invalided out of the army due to their wounds, they were forced to attend lectures on trench warfare. At one of these, Sassoon saw men with amputated limbs and even one blind officer.

The first daytime air raid on London occurred on 13 June, when twenty Gotha bombers dropped more than 100 bombs on the capital.

There were originally twenty-two Gotha bombers ordered to take off to bomb London. A few of them never reached their target due to technical problems. Londoners were still not experienced in air raids. Warnings of a raid often involved someone driving around in a car with a sign saying 'Take cover'.

The raid led to the highest death toll from a single raid in the First World War, when 162 people died. The raid began with bombs being dropped on the docks and the East End. A number of buildings were damaged, including the Royal Hospital Chelsea and the Royal Mint. The greatest tragedy in the early raids was when a bomb fell on Upper North Street School in Poplar, killing eighteen children.

The most serious loss of life on the railway during the raid occurred at Liverpool Street station just before midday. Three of the bombs landed on the station – one on Platform 9 and one on a passenger train that was just about to depart. The third bomb didn't explode. Many of the bombs landed around the station, causing a great deal of damage. The station had been called Bishopsgate until 1909, but had been renamed after Lord Liverpool. In 1912, it had become the eastern terminus of the London Underground, where the Central Line ended.

The writer A.C. Benson, who wrote the words for 'Land of Hope and Glory', witnessed the aftermath of the bombing. He arrived on a delayed train from Cambridge. He saw ambulances and a large silent crowd who were pale but not panicking. He also saw a shrouded figure being carried out of the station.

Benson wasn't the only writer there. Siegfried Sassoon was also there spending time back in London after his time at the front. He was about to enter a bank in Old Broad Street when he realised that there was an air raid taking place. Although a number of female staff ran out of the bank, the cashier he went to carried on and cashed his cheque. Sassoon described him as having made up his mind to go down with his ship, more indignant than afraid of being blown up in his own bank.

On reaching the station, Sassoon saw that a bomb had hit the front carriage of the Cambridge train, the one he had planned to take. He noticed that the clock said 11.50 but that railway time had been interrupted for once in its career. He saw an old man who had died being wheeled away on a porter's barrow, women covered in blood, and occupied train carriages that had been flattened to the tracks. In his *Memoirs of an*

Infantry Officer he said: 'In a trench one was acclimatised to the notion of being exterminated and there was a sense of organised retaliation. But here one was helpless, an invisible enemy spinning down in fine weather.'

Despite his experience of being at the front and seeing men die, he said that he felt sick at the sight of the air raid. The sort of danger during a raid seemed to demand a quality of courage not dissimilar to front-line fortitude. Sassoon was obviously not put out for long. Once he had determined that trains may not be running from the station for some time, he went to St Pancras, where he managed to catch a train to Cambridge.

Sassoon seemed to have an understanding of the railway system. Not long afterwards, he found himself at Crewe station on the way to a posting in Ireland. It was midnight when he was waiting for the Holyhead express to arrive. The people on the platform had 'dead faces' while gloom, vapour and bright lights intermingled above them. Sassoon said that everyone on Crewe station seemed to be eternally condemned to the task of winning the war by moving men, munitions and material to the places appointed for them.

Despite the struggles that the railways in Britain were experiencing in having to cope with the number of men they had lost, even more were about to go. Another 15,000 men from the railway companies had been released for military service. The War Office were looking for another 500,000 men and after some debate it was agreed that the chosen railwaymen would be released from their companies by the end of July.

There had also been some dispute over men being released from the docks for military service. Dockers were often militant when it came to their rights. These problems had finally been sorted out and the unions concerned were co-operating with the military authorities.

Meanwhile in France, it would seem that the use of railways was not going well. According to the *Great War Magazine*, Canadian railway troops were sent to France not at the request of the British but at the request of the Canadian soldiers already serving there as infantry. Every Canadian railroad expert who visited the front in the early days of the war had been appalled by the wasteful methods of conveyance used. Large numbers of heavy trucks were distributing supplies and there was little use of the French railway lines.

The Canadians said that one train could hold as many as 200 trucks and employed four men instead of 400. The Canadian men had been pointing this out continuously, with little encouragement. Finally, Lord Shaughnessy, the president of the Canadian Pacific Railway, who lost his son in the war, recruited a Canadian Railway Battalion and sent it to France.

The Canadians led the way in showing how useful light railways were. The British railway units had built standard gauge lines to large supply dumps but the light railways could carry supplies right up to the front lines. The Canadians had built thousands of miles of light railways in Canada and were now doing the same in France.

It appeared at first as if the Canadian battalion would not be allowed to do anything, but then Lloyd George, Minister of War, appointed Eric Campbell Geddes, later Sir Eric, to reorganise and extend the system of constructing and operating the military railways in France. From that moment, the Canadians came into their own. More battalions were raised and Mr Jack Stewart became Brigadier General of the Canadian railwaymen.

The Canadians boasted that they followed behind the fighting army. A few days after the capture of Vimy, railways had been run right up to the new positions. Light railways were later followed by standard gauge lines. The railway troops worked under constant shellfire while armoured locomotives brought up materials. Sometimes they only worked at night. A mile of track a day could be laid by 600 men and in one case, a bridge 140 feet long was begun on a Friday and completed by the following Tuesday.

It may not have been common knowledge but *The Times* reported on the Canadian light railway builders who, according to the report, had been building strategic lines of all gauges for over a year. At first they were bothered by shells but by this point the Germans had discovered that it was cheaper for us to repair the lines than it was for them to shell it. The Canadians now worked night and day, whatever the weather, supported by the British labour battalions.

Before the advance in July they had been under constant fire, leading to one battalion being shelled out of its headquarters. They had still managed to build the spur lines to get the big guns in place for the morning of the attack. The adequate equipment they had was thanks to the sacrifices of the British and Canadian railways who supplied the materials they needed. The junctions and stations of the new lines were named after the places where the material was torn up from months before in Canada.

At the Yser Canal, the Canadians were helping the Royal Engineers to build new wooden bridges, strong enough to take the heaviest artillery and rolling stock. The timbers were sawn and shaped in a Canadian mill right under the nose of the enemy. The sawyers still wore Stetsons and the style of clothes of the woods they came from.

At the same time as the Canadians were working on railways, the Americans had begun to arrive in France. They set up their own docks, warehouses, storage and railways. The first order for equipment involved 300 locomotives and 150,000 tons of rails. The locomotives came from Baldwin's and the American Locomotive Works. The order was made on 17 July and the first engine was ready in early August. The locomotives were sent over from America intact.

There was also an order for 17,000 French type cars, which were four-wheeled and could carry 10 tons. They then decided to go for American type cars with eight wheels that could carry 33 tons. The order was reduced to 6,000 cars, which were sent in kit form and were assembled on arrival. There had also been orders for railway trucks and locomotives for Russia but after the fall of Alexander Kerensky's government they were not sent and they were used in France instead.

The Americans had formed an organisation of railway instructors for the Trans-Siberian Railway. They were organised on military lines but were not members of the American Army. There were 288 members who sailed to Vladivostok. Due to the situation in Russia, they quickly left again.

The railways that did exist in the crisis-wrought state of Russia were still in use. The revolution led to a phase known as the 'railway war', when trainloads of revolutionary soldiers would travel to an area where there was no support for the revolution and forcibly put down any opposition. If the Allies had continued to send equipment it would have aided these tactics.

The air raids at home continued into August and one area to be attacked was Southend. Twelve aircraft assaulted the town when it was full of holidaymakers and twenty-three people died. One victim of the raid was a Mrs Pond from Brentwood, who was the wife of a serving gunner. She had spent the day at Southend with her 2-year-old daughter.

Mrs Pond had returned to the GER station to catch the 6.15 train back to Brentwood. Aircraft were circling overhead but there was no panic as

Figure 106 Brake vans were an important component of goods trains; the trucks often did not have their own braking system.

they were thought to be British. As the train waited to depart, a bomb fell. Passengers got off the train and ran into the waiting room, where a bomb landed by the window and killed seven people.

A soldier and a sailor who had been on the train tried to get everyone outside and they told them to lie down. They forced some people onto the ground who were trying to run away. More bombs fell outside the station and passengers who arrived after the raid said that they had to step over bodies.

The raid was reported in *The Times* a few days later and the report said that the planes had been heading for London but were attacked by British planes and so dropped their bombs on Southend. Two of the Gothas were shot down. One British pilot described how he shot down a German plane which crashed into the sea with a crew member hanging onto the tail. He then threw the German a lifebelt and tried to signal his position to naval ships.

There had been rumours of Russian troops arriving in the UK throughout the war, all of which were untrue. In August, however, Russian troops did arrive in the country but not hundreds of thousands – just a few thousand. In the later stages of the war, Invergordon in the Highland area of Scotland had become an arrival port for goods from Russia.

The Kerensky government had sent 3,000 Russian troops as a goodwill gesture to fight alongside their Western allies. The Russians were sent south by train along with 300 refugees, no doubt pro-Czarists escaping the revolution. Refugees and assorted nationalities of troops continued to arrive at Invergordon from Russia during the war and beyond it.

Each mile of the front needed between 7 and 10 miles of narrow gauge railway to supply it. The engines were either steam or petrol driven, the petrol ones of course being less visible to the enemy as they approached the front. They were used to bring up supplies and ammunition and could even carry troops, both fit and wounded.

Although the Canadians had led the way in building light railways, the British finally got into the task of building them as well. To run trains of the narrow gauge tracks, hundreds of locomotives were needed. These were built by companies such as Hunslet, Kerr Stuart, Alco, Davenport, Motor Rail and Baldwin's. Converted Model T Ford motor cars were also used as transport running on the railway lines. Close to the front, there was greater use of diesel engines to avoid the danger of steam engine emissions giving away the trains' position to the enemy.

Although it had taken the British much longer than the others involved in the war to discover the usefulness of light railways, by the end of 1917 there were nearly 1,000 locomotives and 5,000 wagons in use on the Western Front. Not only did their use remove the need for dangerously large stores of shells near the front but they were also used to deliver water in tanks as well as to carry the wounded back from the front to hospitals in the rear. King George V was given a tour of the front on a narrow gauge rail car.

In September, there was a terrible end for some of the soldiers who had travelled across the world from New Zealand to help fight in the war. On the 24th of the month, a train carrying New Zealand troops stopped at Bere Ferrers near Plymouth. A number of the men got out of the wrong side of the train just as an express train came along, killing ten of them. The accident did not arouse as much press interest as train crashes usually did.

The public at home were beginning to experience the effects of the war by this time, especially in London. Airplanes had replaced the Zeppelins on bombing raids, which had become more intense on the city. When the police drove round in cars with 'Take cover' placards, it was common for the population to use the London Underground tunnels as shelters.

Figure 107 Birkenhead station, from where many American troops were carried south by the GWR after arriving at Liverpool.

Towards the end September, there were raids on two nights running, on the 24th and 25th. Rather than running to an emergency shelter when a raid occurred, families began to move into the tunnels of the Underground in the evening before a raid began, taking their bedding, food and even pets with them. Pets were later banned from entry.

Many of those who were sheltering then spent their time riding on the trains instead of just staying in the station, especially on the Circle Line. There were even trains that were berthed specifically for their use. More than 4 million people used the Underground for shelters during the war.

In many cases, there were no special arrangements for passengers on the main line railways in the event of an air raid. At Euston, the L&NWR thought that the station was so close to parts of the Underground that passengers could make their own way to a place of safety. This also applied to most of the staff.

Some staff were, however, expected to stay at their post during raids. These were workers in the telephone exchange and anyone involved in the air raid defence system. Everyone else could head towards the Underground or the station basements. As the raids became more frequent, parts of the telephone exchange were moved to more secure positions that were better protected.

Euston was quite lucky to escape any serious damage from air raids; this was despite appearing on the damage list five times. The damage was mainly broken glass or roof slates. On 29 September, there were sixty-five sheets of glass broken in the roof at the station but this was due to shrapnel from anti-aircraft guns rather than directly from the bombing.

During a raid the following day at the Camden Depot, a shell from an anti-aircraft gun broke six panes of glass in the roof and fell into a wagon full of naval overcoats. It was removed unexploded. Another shell made a hole in the ground 8 feet deep but also did not explode. There seemed to be a large number of shells from anti-aircraft guns and bombs from enemy aircraft that did not explode – otherwise damage and fatalities could have been much worse.

The discussion on whether the government should keep control of the railways after the war was raised again by the Railway Executive Committee in late 1917. They came to the conclusion that this would not be possible without further legislation. The idea was not going away, however.

The raids continued into October and on the 19th of the month, the L&NWR was again the victim when twelve bombs fell on Northampton on or near the company lines. Seven of the bombs fell between the fences each side of the line; six of these were incendiaries. The only damage was to a fence. Sadly, one incendiary fell on a company house in Park Street, killing the wife of a company bricklayer and one of their children.

The death of anyone during the raids was a terrible tragedy but considering the number of raids that took place during the war, the railway system escaped with very few serious problems. Much of the damage caused was able to be repaired very quickly and in most cases did not seem to have led to any lengthy delay in the running of the railways.

Chapter 5

1918

The January issue of *The War Illustrated* included a report on wartime wages and price increases. The report mentioned how many men had gone to serve their country while those who stayed at home had benefited by the great demand for labour. It claimed that 4 million men had left to fight but by the previous September, only 1.265 million had been replaced by women.

The shortage of labour had led to a great increase in wages in most industries, including the railways. War bonuses and overtime had raised wages in some cases by 100 per cent. The rise in wages had, according to the report, led to a rise in prices for many commodities such as transport.

January was a bad month for accidents on the railway. This was the third January out of the last four years to see fatal crashes. On the 19th of the month, at Little Salkeld, 15 miles south of Carlisle, a Scottish express from London to Glasgow ran into part of a cutting that had collapsed onto the line. There were seven deaths.

The driver had seen the bank begin to collapse as he approached it. He applied the brake but couldn't stop in time. The engine mounted the bank and caused the first carriage to telescope into the tender. As with the other accidents during the war, there were soldiers on the train who helped with the rescue, and the injured were taken to Fusehill Military Hospital in Carlisle.

Former railwaymen were common in the Royal Engineers. Lance Corporal E. Phillips RE had been a relaying labourer at Newton Abbot in Devon. He was awarded the Military Medal and was mentioned in Sir John French's despatch in January. Captain H.T. Rendall had worked at the Motor Car Department at Slough and had also been a pupil of the Engineering Department at Swindon. He had previously worked in America on railway engineering and been a reserve officer in the Mechanical Transport Branch of the Army Service Corps. Summoned to

Aldershot at the outbreak of war, he later became Inspector of Mechanical Transport of the Army in the Field.

The use of train ferries was hardly known in the UK before the war apart from a few attempts at their use in Scotland, but these were just for river crossing. The use of train ferries was common in other parts of the world. It was claimed that the idea for their use in crossing the Channel was put forward to the government in late 1916 by Mr Follett Holt, Chairman of the British-owned Entre Ríos Railways in Argentina, which had used ferries.

The idea seemed to be an ideal way to move equipment across the Channel and three ferries were built under orders from the government. Two were built by Armstrong Whitworth and one by Fairfield Shipbuilding and Engineering. A fourth was added – an ex-train ferry that had been in use in Canada crossing the St Lawrence River at Quebec. They ran from Southampton and Richborough throughout 1918 and into 1919. The one at Southampton was sited west of the Royal Pier and had its own marshalling yard.

Richborough is at the mouth of the Stour River and had been a port as far back as Roman times. A new port had been built earlier in the war for cross-Channel barges and began operating in December 1916. The barges could cross to France and travel along French canals to get closer to the front.

The ferries were run by merchant seamen and retired naval men who were enlisted into the Inland Waterways and Docks section of the Royal Engineers. They wore army uniforms and were given army ranks. After the war the ferries came under the control of the SE&CR but were still owned by the War Office.

Liverpool had been a busy port throughout the war for both the import of goods and the arrival of soldiers from overseas. The year 1916 had been a hectic time and 1917 had seen even more arrivals from Canada, Australia and New Zealand. The first Americans also arrived in the country and all had been dealt with by the L&NWR.

The coming of the new year was to see an even greater increase in the arrival of military men from overseas. As well as over 700,000 American troops there were still Canadians, Australians and even large numbers of Chinese labourers coming to work on the Western Front. Where previously the L&NWR had managed to carry all the arrivals away from

Figure 108 The war memorial at King's Cross was originally erected in 1920 with the names of 937 men of the GNR who died in the war. The original memorial was replaced in 1973 by this modern one.

Liverpool, the numbers were now too great for them to cope with alone. The other railways that served Liverpool now began to help. The L&YR, the GCR, the Midland and the GWR from Birkenhead all played their part.

Even then, with all these companies involved it was difficult to move all the men away from Liverpool as soon as they arrived. The answer was to open a rest camp in the area where the arrivals could spend some time while waiting to be moved. The camp was built by the Knotty Ash Cheshire lines station. It began as a tented camp but huts were built later.

There had been talks taking place about the end of the war as early as January 1918. A discussion in the Commons in mid-January raised the topic of reconstruction after the war. Dr Christopher Addison, the Minister for Reconstruction, said that in some industries there would be a shortage of raw materials as well as transport. He went on to say that works that supplied machinery were already full of foreign orders. Large sums of money had been paid to ensure that these foreign orders took priority.

Dr Addison went on to say that there was going to be a prodigious demand for railway equipment after the war as Britain's railways had had hardly any renewals of equipment since the war began. This also applied to India and the colonies, as well as the areas devastated by the war. One answer to this would be to avoid the scandals that had happened in the past regarding the disposal of war stores by using the light railway equipment from the battlefields as a means of transport in rural areas at home. Despite the discussion about the demand for reconstruction there were still calls for more men to enlist in the army in late January and the Schedule of Protected Occupations was being revised for those employed in munitions and in railway workshops. One plan was to increase the age of munitions workers allowed to join up; if they were over 32 years of age, they were now to be liable for recruitment.

There were attempts to change the status of skilled men so as to make them available for recruitment. This led to disputes with the unions, including the railwaymen's unions, who argued that men who had been upgraded during the war should not now be seen as unskilled. The Ministry of National Service seemed to agree with the unions to some extent, stating that it was impossible to apply a general scheme to the whole country and that the only solution was to deal with the position shop by shop.

There were a number of appeals regarding protected occupations in the printed schedule relating to them. One example was of an engine driver at an important experimental agricultural station. The man's application to avoid enlistment was on the grounds that he was indispensable, mainly due to the number of men from the station who had already been called up, but he also had special knowledge of experimental plots. His application was not successful as he was only given a three-month delay so that a substitute could be found. It is hard to see how he could be more important to the army than he was in his civilian position.

Whilst the government were trying to enlist more men from munitions and railway work into the forces, women workers in these industries were being dismissed. Winston Churchill was at a meeting at the Ministry of

Munitions in late February to discuss with the unions the recent large-scale dismissals of women workers. Workers were supposed to be given two weeks' notice, which hadn't always been done, and in one case a factory had completely shut down with all the staff losing their jobs.

There had been some dispute between the government and the railways in regard to some of the work that went on during the war. This was evident in the provision of railway lines to military camps as sometimes the military had to pay for their own lines. In 1918, the War Office requested that the railway companies become responsible for working and repairing the railway lines serving military camps. At this point there were about fourteen camps with railway lines in Britain.

The War Office were still constructing lines to new camps, some of which were for the American troops arriving in the country. The lines serving the camps were not always exclusive to the military. At Codford Camp there was a track just over 4 miles long but more than 2 miles of this was part of the main line.

The use of railways by the Germans at the beginning of the war has already been discussed. Towards the end of 1917, however, they had another large military transport task to fulfil. After Russia had pulled out of the war late in the previous year, the Germans had begun to move many of their troops from the Eastern Front to the Western Front.

When Germany and Russia agreed the Treaty of Brest-Litovsk in March, the Germans began to move many more men. According to Major General Max Hoffman, once the treaty was signed everything that could possibly be moved was loaded onto trains and transported to the west. The Germans used their railway planning to move about forty divisions in an attempt to win the war before a large number of Americans arrived.

After the slow start, the Royal Engineers and railway companies had laid hundreds of miles of standard and light railway tracks during the war. More British locomotives arrived in France as the war went on. Twelve of the British railway companies supplied 600 locomotives. They were mainly 0-6-0s and were generally very old. The GCR supplied nineteen that were modern. The GWR supplied eleven that were brand new along with eighty-four old six-wheelers. There were also 300 Ministry of Munitions 2-8-0s. Most of these came over on railway ferries. There were also 500 American locomotives, including 150 2-8-0 Baldwins.

Toll for the Brave.

"When can their glory fade!"—Tennyson.

The following brave Great Eastern Railway men have lost their lives in their Country's service :—

MR. ALBERT ISAACS, who has been employed as a bricklayer's labourer at Colchester, was called to the Royal Fleet Reserve on 3rd August. Mr. Issacs entered the service in October, 1908, after serving in the Royal Navy as A.B. for 12 years.

He was one of the crew of the ill-fated H.M.S. Hogue. Mr. Isaacs was a general favourite amongst his mates.

MR. A. ISAACS.

♦   ♦   ♦

MR. WILLIAM MITCHELL, who was a permanent way labourer in the Engineer's Department at Cambridge, was called up to his regiment the 2nd Essex, at the commencement of the war. He was killed in action on the 13th September, whilst serving with the expeditionary force in France. Mr. Mitchell leaves a wife and one child.

MR. W. MITCHELL.

♦   ♦   ♦

MR. W. NICHOLS, who had been employed as a platelayer at Ipswich, Lower Yard since July, 1908, was called up to the Royal Navy at the commencement of the war. He was one of the crew of the ill-fated H.M.S. Aboukir, sunk in the North Sea on the 22nd of September. Mr. Nichols belonged to the Royal Naval Reserve as 1st class stoker, and was 38 years of age.

MR. W. NICHOLS.

♦   ♦   ♦

POLICE CONSTABLE WILLIAM HENRY WILSON, Liverpool Street, who was a reservist of the Royal West Kent Regiment, was killed in action on August 23rd. He had only been in the Company's Police Force about eighteen months.

His brother, who was serving with the Oxford Light Infantry, has also been killed in action.

MR. W. H. WILSON.

MR. ARTHUR ROGERS, who lost his life while serving as an able seaman on board the ill-fated H.M.S. Cressy, was a porter at Devonshire St. (Goods). He was born in October 21st, 1882, and entered the service on February 27th, 1913. His previous naval service was on board torpedo boat No. 17, and on H.M.S. "Cæsar."

He was a good worker and was held in high esteem by his colleagues.

MR. A. ROGERS.

♦   ♦   ♦

GUNNER J. ADAMS, 29th Battery, R.F.A., who was killed in action at Brenelle on September 13th, was in the service of the G.N., G.C., and G.E., Cartage Committee. He only entered the service in March, 1914, and, being an army reservist, was called to the colours on August 4th.

MR. J. ADAMS.

♦   ♦   ♦

MR. C. E. WITH, porter, entered the service at Bishopsgate in March this year. Mr. With was on service with the colours in the 2nd Royal Scots Regiment when he was killed.

MR. C. E. WITH.

♦   ♦   ♦

MR. JOHN EDWIN HULL, of the Royal Naval Reserve, who has been killed in action, was a porter at Goodman's Yard. He entered the Company's service as recently as November, 1913.

♦   ♦   ♦

MR. T. FLOREY, porter at Ipswich, entered the service in October, 1909, and was serving with the colours in the 3rd Signal Company of the Royal Engineers at the time of his death.

Figure 109 A page from the *Great Eastern Railway Magazine* showing some of their employees who made the ultimate sacrifice.

It was London's railway stations that suffered the most damage from air raids as well as the most deaths. Five bombs fell on St Pancras near the station and hotel; only four of the bombs exploded. The raid, which took place on 17 March, killed twenty people. The majority of these were sheltering under a covered carriage drive leading from the station to the hotel. One of the platforms was destroyed. It was to result in the greatest number of deaths in any attack on a London station in the war. The deaths included eight Midland Railway employees.

In March, the LNWR workshop at Crewe became His Majesty's Number 9 munitions store. As well as munitions, they produced 138 of the Crewe Tractors that were being used on the light railways in France. The workshop also made artificial limbs for servicemen who had lost them to wounds.

There was more news of the L&NWR in their *Railway Gazette* in April. There was a report that Second Lieutenant Hugh Douglas Bird, Royal Fusiliers, had been killed in action in March. Bird was a member of the Sportsman's Battalion, a special unit that had originally been recruited amongst sportsmen and men from the world of entertainment. Because of their fitness they had been allowed to recruit up to the age of 45 early in the war, before the age of entry was raised. Bird had been educated at the Central Foundation School London and had then joined the L&NWR in the estate department at Euston. At the outbreak of war he had joined the Queen Victoria Rifles and been promoted to sergeant before being commissioned in the Sportsman's Battalion in May 1917. He had been awarded the Military Cross at Buckingham Palace in December 1917.

The report went on to say that he had been killed by a shell on 25 March. A telegram was sent to his wife informing her of his death and a memorial service was held at Stanmore Church. The final sentence of the report stated that since it had been written, there was reasonable hope that Bird was in fact a prisoner of war.

A report in *The Times* in April discussed the continuing conflict between the needs of the railways and the forces when it came to manpower. The enlistment of railway workers had been carefully regulated, with men who enlisted without permission being classed as having left the railway service and lost all privileges and allowances. The removal of young men from the railways had gone on throughout the war until by early 1918, there were 170,000 railwaymen serving in the forces.

Figure 110 War memorial at Attenborough station (Nottinghamshire) for the station staff who died in the war. Their regiments are listed but none were members of railway units.

Many of those who did enlist, such as porters and ticket inspectors, were easily replaced by women. The report went on to say that it was doubtful if the further removal of men from the railways could so easily be remedied. One option was to replace young men with older men who were released from military service who were no longer fit. The increase of age for military service to 51 in 1918 was not thought to have had a great effect on the railways as most men of over 43 in railway employment were engaged in work of great responsibility and could not be replaced.

There was still some level of dispute over what was essential work. It was the Ministry of National Service's view that countrywide revisions of what was essential work were not possible and seemed to apply especially to the railways. It was decided that this would definitely have to be based on a shop-by-shop approach. Such widespread reform of what was an essential occupation could have led to the destruction of the efficient running of the railway system in the country.

Surely deciding what was essential work on a shop-by-shop basis would have led to some level of uncertainty. Would an essential worker in one shop be seen as non-essential in another, even if both were doing the same job?

Theft from the railways had been a problem throughout the war, just as it was in peacetime. What was surprising in a case of theft in May was the time that the thieves had worked for the railway. Edward Paisley, a foreman shunter, had worked for the GNR for twenty-eight years; Ernest Buck, a shunter, and Frederick Padley, an assistant shunter, had worked for the company for ten and six years respectively. The three men were each sentenced to six months' imprisonment for stealing a number of bottles of whisky from a railway truck. The theft took place at the company's Hornsey sidings. It seems quite strange that they would risk what had been a long career for what was essentially petty theft.

On 19/20 May, a Gotha aircraft dropped a 100kg bomb on the railway lines near Wanstead Station in East London; it damaged the lines and fifty nearby houses. A bomb also landed on railway lines near Kentish Town and despite not exploding, it damaged the lines near Grafton Road. It was to be the last bombing raid of the war.

The railway companies had been building hospital trains throughout the war and in May a new GWR train went on display at Paddington. According to a report in *The Times*, the train would be used in Italy. Red Cross officials were present to instruct the public on the train's features. It would also go on shown in Birmingham and Bristol. It was described as similar to the train built by the Midland Railway Company for the American Army a few months before. Certain mechanical modifications had been made, suggested by recent experience to make it the latest, most modern hospital on wheels. It was painted khaki outside and white inside. The sixteen coaches provided accommodation for 342 cot patients as well as areas for infectious and mental cases in special isolation wards. The officers' section had dining and sitting compartments.

The windows were fitted with louvre blinds covered with wire netting to keep out flies. The ventilation and sanitation were based on the most approved principles. The train carried 3,000 gallons of water, and 50 gallons of hot water could be supplied at any time. It had electric lights, electric fans and was steam-heated. There was a special steam heating system that could be operated even when the locomotive was not attached.

Although separate sections for mental cases were mentioned, there seems to be no indication on whether the hospital trains that went on display contained a special cells compartment. These were padded cells for those suffering from shell shock and would perhaps not be something that the makers would have wanted to be seen by the public.

In early 1918, a new danger swept the country that was to have a more deadly effect than air raids on the population. It was also to cause problems in raising new recruits. What eventually became known as Spanish Flu began to prove fatal to large numbers of people. Due to the fact that the war was still on, censorship was still in force, which prevented a lot of the publicity that may have helped to inform people about the danger of infection. The flu was to come in three waves over the following years and it was estimated that more than 50 million people died from it worldwide.

The press had begun to report on the flu from the middle of the year but were calling it the Spanish Epidemic, which *The Times* reported as appearing in Madrid and spreading with remarkable rapidity. It is now understood that the virus was first observed in the US but wartime censorship initially surpressed its reporting in the countries involved in the war so as not to affect morale. It was, however, reported freely by the Spanish press as they were a neutral country and not subject to the censors, and this resulted in it being called the Spanish Flu. It was already causing problems in barracks, schools and factories in Spain and transport had been affected due to lack of workers.

By July, *The Times* was reporting on cases in the United Kingdom, schools were being closed and business was being severely hampered. In

Birmingham, one doctor found 178 patients waiting for him at his surgery. The flu was affecting production for the war; in munitions factories, ironworks and railway workshops, many of the workers were being sent home, some in ambulances owing to how suddenly the symptoms struck.

In Manchester, sixty tramway drivers and guards were off work as well as many railwaymen. The rate of infection was also having a devastating effect on the mines. One Newcastle colliery had eighteen underground workers off on one day, and in Nottinghamshire, one pit lost 250 men in a day, leading to reduced coal production, which would have a serious effect on the railways.

The flu pandemic itself also had a great impact on the railways and some of the rail unions were able to help the families of those workers who lost their lives due to the illness. The National Union of Railwaymen kept detailed records of their members who died in service. In many cases, a flu victim's cause of death was recorded as pneumonia. As the flu became more common, cause of death was often given as flu *and* pneumonia.

What is interesting about the figures is the ages of those dying from the flu. The majority of them were younger men under the age of 40; indeed, many were under 30. One theory as to why this was the case is that older people had lived through previous flu epidemics and may have had some level of resistance to the new form of the illness. Of course, medical practice at this time was not far enough advanced to be able to understand and deal with such viruses, so this was just a theory.

One hypothesis about the spread of the flu was that it was that it was circulated by servicemen returning from France while crowded together in trains. This could also be an explanation as to why so many railway employees died as they would have been dealing with the men who were on the trains that they were working on.

Many of the hardest hit towns in the UK were in ports and coastal areas, which seems to support the theory that it was spread by returning servicemen. The armed forces were monitoring the flu. Walter Morley Fletcher, who was on the Army Pathological Committee, asked that details of the spread of the infection should be sent to the *British Medical Journal*. A later report by Sir Arthur Newsome, of the General Medical Council, was written for the Royal Society of Medicine. In the report Sir Arthur said that he issued a memo in early 1918 advising people to stay at home to avoid catching the flu. He advised against large gatherings and the overcrowding of public transport such as trains.

Sir Arthur's advice was not seen as being in the public interest. The government decided that the war effort was more important than public health and suppressed the memo. This was despite crowded troop trains and large armament factories being ideal sites for the spread of the disease. Of course, not having the troops moved or the shells manufactured would have been even more of a disaster in their eyes. The government did little to warn the public of the ways to resist the illness until after the war ended.

To be fair to the government, the flu did seem to have been dying out by the summer but as winter approached, there was a new wave of infection after large crowds gathered to celebrate the end of the war and the crowded troop trains returned from France. The flu claimed over 200,000 deaths in the UK alone.

Although the war may not have been the cause of the epidemic it certainly helped to spread it. Large numbers of the country's medical professionals had been sent overseas due to the war, leaving a shortage of doctors at home – not that there was an effective treatment they could have employed anyway. Action in Britain seemed to be based on advice such as that in the local newspaper. One local newspaper in Bexhill-on-Sea advised people to take later trains to work so as to avoid crowds. *The Perthshire Advertiser* claimed that there were more stringent laws regarding the health of animals than there were relating to people.

There was no general countrywide response to the pandemic as each area was left to its own devices and advice such as 'smoke more and eat onions' were of little help to the population. Many other countries seemed to take more serious steps to stop the spread of the disease. In America people had to have a signed certificate to be able to travel by train; in Spain, train passengers were sprayed with disinfectant.

By the middle of the year, there was a serious shortage of spare parts for all railway stock. There were no new locomotives being built and very little maintenance was being carried out on existing stock. Francis Dent, the General Manager of the SE&CR and a member of the Railway Executive Committee, was sent to America. He took with him Mr Bowen Cooke, Chief Mechanical Engineer of the L&NWR, and Mr A.J. Hill, Chief Mechanical Engineer of the GER. They were on a special mission and managed to buy some spares.

Figure 111 British Royal Artillery gunners loading pontoon boats on the Scarpe River with shells near a light railway engine passing on the line near Saint-Laurent-Blangy, France, 22 April 1917 during the Battle of Arras. It looks as though goods were transferred between the two forms of transport. (*George Grantham Bain Collection/Library of Congress*)

The hospital trains carrying the wounded from France had to deal with a wide variety of wounds and different levels of injury. The wards on the trains had facilities for those who needed to lie flat and those who could sit up. *The War Illustrated* of June showed images of the wards, which included nurses holding caged canaries whose singing was hoped to cheer up the wounded men.

The report went on to describe Villiers Street in London, which had achieved a new importance since the war began. It had once been known for having the largest billiard saloon in London, but by this time it was known for something else. It seems that both day and night, the street was full of motor ambulances awaiting the arrival of the wounded from France. The injured men were loaded into the ambulances from the entrance to Charing Cross station in Villiers Street. Each vehicle took four patients to hospitals in various parts of London.

Despite all the publicity, hospital trains were not always as good as the hype that surrounded them. Those who were lucky enough to get a place on a hospital train were the most likely to survive; the wounded who had little chance of living were normally left in France. It was the Royal Army Medical Corps that was responsible for the trains and each one was commanded by an RAMC major. Although they had operating theatres, advanced procedures were not carried out on trains unless it was an emergency.

When hospital trains went on display they had nurses and first aid staff, but on a working train there may only have been three nurses and three doctors for more than 500 men. Because of the shortages of staff they would frequently work through the night. The staff quarters were often filled with the overflow of the wounded. One nurse wrote in a letter: 'Imagine a hospital as big as King's College all packed into a train.' In some cases, staff 'lived' on the trains for years.

By 1918, there was severe strain on the US transport system in France. There were never enough yards and junctions for supplies, and those that were in existence were overworked. Locomotive drivers often toiled for eighteen hours a day and there were a number of accidents due to tiredness. This was despite the presence of 50,000 US Transport Corps men.

There were also 250 ex-Belgian railway locomotives operating in France during the war. They had been evacuated when the Germans invaded in 1914. Many of these had been used by the Railway Operating Division and two of the 0-6-0s were repaired at Stratford in London before returning to France.

By August, the discussions on what would happen to the railways after the war had become more intense. A select Committee on Transport said that the railways could not be allowed to return to the pre-war system. They maintained that a temporary period was not good enough; they wanted complete unification under either public or private hands.

The Times of 17 September published a report from Fred James, the official correspondent with the Canadian forces in France. James wrote that the Canadian and British railway troops were following on the heels of the advancing artillery and infantry. Canadian troops were distributed according to demand from north of Ypres to the furthest point south where the British were fighting. They were also working in one French sector.

The work of the Canadians included laying new lines and repairing damaged ones captured from the Germans. They were also involved in building new bridges, switches for big guns and sidings for ammunition. When the enemy blew up a railway bridge while retreating, the Canadians were rushed to the area when it looked as though the British advance would be held up. They repaired the bridge within forty-eight hours.

Not all the work went on behind the lines. At one point, the Germans were forced to abandon some rolling stock, including an engine and a number of cars. The Canadians went and got steam up in the engine and took about a dozen of the cars to the rear. The next night they went back in the stolen engine and took the remaining the cars under German shellfire.

While fighting still continued into September there were strikes going on at home, including a number on the railways. At one point in September, the government threatened strikers with conscription. They were told to work or fight. Mr G.H. Roberts, the Minister for Labour, returned from a tour of France in September, during which he discussed the strikes with the men at the front.

Roberts said that he found the men in a wonderful spirit and was often asked about preparations for the end of the war and reconstruction. He was also asked a number of questions about the strikes at home. Many of the men believed that the strikes had led to delays in the arrival of necessary munitions. Roberts refused to admit that this was the case but did seem to believe what the men were saying. There were often comments from men during meetings asking workers back home to keep on working until the war was won.

In October, when it was becoming clear that the war was close to its end, Sir Herbert Walker, the acting chairman of the Railway Executive Committee and a member of the Select Committee on transport, said that the Highland Railway had had more heavy burdens thrown at it than any other company.

The company route, which started at Perth, was jointly owned with the NBR and the Caledonian Railway. It was the Highland Railway that got all the accumulated traffic from the main lines from the south for lines beyond Inverness. The company had only 485 miles of track and more than 400 miles of it were single lines. The ground that the Highland ran on was such rough terrain, with mountains and numerous bridges, that it was often too expensive to lay double tracks.

There was of course another problem – that of the weather in the Highlands. Much of the track had snow fences alongside built from old sleepers, which went some way to stop snow drifting onto the lines. Many of the trains had to run with snow ploughs on the front but still often had to be dug out when the weather was too fierce. Much of the company's pre-war work had been in the summer for pleasure and the winter had been used for maintenance. During the war they had to work all year round.

Their main duties were to Scapa Flow with supplies for the fleet, and to Invergordon to send supplies to Russia up to the revolution, and these were year-round tasks. When troops were sent to protect the area they were based in tents, which had not been the best form of living conditions in that climate. Later, huts were built for them.

Running all year round had been difficult for the Highland Railway, so much so that none of their maintenance engineers had been allowed to be called up. The company had 152 locomotives and of these, fifty had to eventually be withdrawn while another fifty were on their last legs. They had to borrow locomotives and fitters from other railway companies to keep the lines running. Towards the end of the war, they were even short of signalmen and some loops had to be shut down.

It seems fitting that as the railways had so much influence on the war and its outcome that the end of the conflict occurred in a railway carriage. The carriage was part of a train that had been used by Marshal Ferdinand Foch. He had been made General in Chief of the Allies in April and had used the train to travel to the front.

The meeting between Foch and the Germans was held in secret on 8 November on the train on a line through the Forest of Compiègne. It was a remote area where the railway lines had been built for French railway guns. The terms offered by Foch included the surrender by the Germans of thousands of railway locomotives as well as other military equipment and occupied land. The fighting ended on 11 November – although it wasn't to be the end for many of the members of the armed forces. As the German Army began to pull back towards home they were followed by the Allies. Part of the agreement was that a large part of Germany would be occupied by the Allies. The war was still not officially over, as Germany had not surrendered. There was a chance that they would continue to fight and the occupation forces were ready for this. It was a reason why many disappointed men still found themselves in uniform.

At home, the railways had spent most of the war carrying troops towards the south from where they could be sent across to France. Now that the fighting was over they were carrying them back – at least the ones who were not still needed. One of the places they were taken to was the demobilisation base at Purfleet on the Thames, in Essex. There had been rifle ranges there used as military camps for many years before the war began.

The men were carried there on the LT&SR line owned by the Midland Railway. Once the men were processed and released, they were once more carried away by train to get them home. Many of them – the lucky ones – were returning to their jobs on the railways.

THE RT HON. WINSTON CHURCHILL.

The NER held good on their promise to reinstate men who had returned fit from the war and they were given their old jobs back. Not all the men came back fit but the NER did their best for those who had been injured as well. A departmental committee found light work positions for over 500 men who were partly incapacitated by war injuries. Those who required special treatment were also looked after.

A number of men who had previously occupied low grade positions with the NER but who had distinguished themselves in the forces, such as those who

Figure 112 Winston Churchill, who made a statement saying that the railways would be nationalised after the war.

reached commissioned rank, were given special training for higher grade jobs.

The General Manager of the L&YR, John Audley Frederick Aspinall, addressed the Institution of Civil Engineers in November. He was speaking on how improvement was needed to increase the economy of railway transport now that the war was over. One of the main points that had to be dealt with was the size of wagons and the different loading gauge of some companies. In the past this had often led to goods being unloaded onto different trucks when meeting a different loading gauge line. Due to the varied ownership of the railways it seems that this was still a problem, albeit on a smaller scale, even after government control during the war.

There were still some small lines that were of a different loading gauge; some of these were connected with mines. This meant that some of the larger wagons could not access all lines. Aspinall went on to argue that the 10-ton wagons used for carrying much of the coal produced should be increased to 20 or even 40-ton capacity. He also argued that private ownership of railway wagons was an unnecessary expense.

Despite criticising the use of different loading gauge tracks he argued that the many hundreds of miles of 60-centimetre tracks used in France should be brought home and re-laid for use as agricultural lines without the restrictions of existing light railway or tramway legislation.

The end of the year was to see a definite mood for the takeover of the railways. In December, Winston Churchill stated that the government policy was based on nationalisation. It seems that Churchill's words were stronger than the action that was actually taken.

Chapter 6

1919

Getting the army across the Channel had been handled well by the British railway system. Now that the war was over, they had to make plans for getting them home. Early in the war, military units such as the Pals battalions would have comprised many men from the same locality, which had a devastating effect on their home town or village for the ones that suffered heavy losses. As the war progressed, however, replacement men had been sent to whichever units were short of bodies, so getting them home again was a more complicated task than it would have been earlier in the war as members of the same units could come from many different parts of the country.

For the task of getting the men home, the country was divided into twenty areas, each with a disposal unit. In this way they could be demobilised as close to where they lived as possible. This would then avoid men being sent all over the country to get home. They were to be sent to rest camps in France, from where they would be sorted into home areas. This would then involve full trains heading to each area from the nearest port to the area camps. The plan was for the railways to deal with nearly 300,000 men a week.

The problem was that the French said they were too busy to run trains from rest camps to separate ports as their railways were already too congested. They would only send troops en masse to the ports that they themselves found the easiest to reach and the men could then be sorted once they were back in England. The railway companies again had to revise their plans to cope with the French intransigence.

The end of the war had still not led to any firm plans on the future of Britain's railways. This was despite the comment made by Winston Churchill at an election meeting that the government plan was to nationalise the railways. There was still no definite evidence that this was actual government policy. Meanwhile, a select committee on transport was recommending unified ownership rather than state acquisition.

There was also some debate between the railway unions and the Railway Executive Committee over the forty-eight-hour week that the government had promised railway workers. The Railway Executive Committee apparently did not have the power to deal with this despite still being in control of the railways. The unions were assured that the forty-eight-hour week would be one of the first measures submitted to the new parliament.

In 1919, the SE&CR built a prototype parcels van, which was to achieve fame as the Cavell Van. It was so called as it was used to bring back the body of Edith Cavell, the nurse executed by the Germans for aiding the escape of Allied prisoners. The van carried her body from Dover to London in May and her remains were reburied at Norwich Cathedral on the 19th of the month.

In July, the coach was also used to carry the body of Captain Charles Fryatt from Dover to London, and a funeral was held for him on the 8th of the month at St Paul's Cathedral before he was transported by train from Liverpool Street station to All Saints' Church, Upper Dovercourt, Essex, where he was finally laid to rest. In 1920, the coach also carried the body of the Unknown Warrior to London for his burial in Westminster Abbey. The van was used by the SE&CR, Southern Railway and British Railway until it was restored in 2010, and is now based at the Kent & East Sussex Railway.

Now that the war was over, much of the wartime railway system was obsolete. This included the railway ferries that had been taking trains across the Channel in the period after the war until the Great Eastern Train Ferries service was established in 1923 in conjunction with Belgian State Railways. They purchased the ferries and moved them to Harwich, which had been used as a naval base during the war. A new service to the Continent was started in 1924 and was taken over by the LNER in the 1930s.

* * *

There is no doubt that the railways played a vital role in the war. Mr Vernon Sommerfield, who was an expert on transport issues, considered rail power a specialised form of military strength. He argued that from a military point of view, railways should be considered in the same way as the navy. Their value in strategical terms was similar and 'rail power' was as justified a term as 'sea power'. This was especially shown in the value of coastal railways for the rapid transportation of troops in the event of an attack – a view that had been evidenced in Germany.

The First World War was the first modern war that had an effect on the population at home, and this included how the railways operated for both civilians and military use. Air raids were a new phenomenon and caused some damage to Britain's railways. They also led to the deaths of a number of railway workers – a total of twenty-four were killed in air raids. Twelve of these were from the GER and ten from the Midland Railway. There were thirty-one air raids on London during the war. The number of employees who were killed while in railway service was very low compared with the numbers who died in the Second World War.

During the war, there were 672 people killed and 1,962 wounded in the United Kingdom by enemy action, bombing and shelling, but these were not all railway related. From July 1917, the London Underground was used for shelter by more than 4 million Londoners on forty occasions. Berthed trains were used on thirty occasions. This was quite low when compared to the extent of their use during the Second World War. Other tunnels under the Thames were also used as shelters in the First World War, such as Blackwell and Rotherhithe, which were banned for such use in the Second World War due to larger and more deadly bombs. Liverpool Street station was bombed twice – in 1915 and 1917.

The railway workers who suffered the most were the ones who enlisted and were sent abroad to fight. About 21,000 railway staff lost their lives in the war serving with the forces after 68,500 women and 184,000 men joined up. By end of 1919, 49 per cent of London Underground workers had enlisted.

The railway workers in the forces who survived the war were among the lucky ones, who often returned home to find that their jobs had been saved. Many others faced unemployment. However, those railway workers who returned to their former jobs were to find a railway system that had a different threat hanging over it than the military one it had just faced.

The railways played another small part in the demobilisation process. Each man was given a final leave of twenty-eight days, during which they could wear civilian clothes. They then had to hand in their greatcoats at a railway station and for this they would receive one pound.

Things were beginning to get back to normal on the railways at home. The railway system had survived in a much better condition than the German and the French railways had as they had been in the centre of the conflict. Although the numbers of locomotives and trucks that had been sent abroad seemed huge, they had only amounted to around 3 per cent of their rolling stock and most of the locomotives were returned.

Despite the pressure the British railway system had endured it had come out of the war in a reasonably stable condition. The biggest problem was the backlog of repairs, and in this respect, some lines were worse off than others. The SE&CR was particularly run down, as was the SWR, which had been responsible for much of the cross-Channel traffic. The GER was coping well though. It had kept some cross-Channel services going throughout the war and quickly reinstated some of the pleasure services.

However, the end of the war posed problems for both the railway workers and the management. Wages had been high during the conflict and now there was the issue of the war bonus and what would happen to it. Employers and the government did not want the bonus to continue or to be added to the standard rate of pay. The feeling of 'all being in it together' was reverting to the 'us and them' status of employer and employed.

When the railway workers came out on strike in 1920 over the loss of wages for the lower paid, the heroes of the railways who had been praised so soundly during the war were suddenly declared to be 'anarchists' and 'Bolsheviks' by the government. It is hard not to suspect that this was a political move meant to induce conflict with the unions and yet the unions came out on top and managed to keep wages at the same level.

Despite an upturn in rail services, great changes were under way. In February 1919, with no consultation with the railway companies, the Ministry of Ways and Communications announced that to improve locomotive transport the government would keep control of the railways for another two years and looked likely to nationalise the system. The two years were to end in August 1921.

There was still no certainty about what was to happen and in September 1919 a new ministry took over from the Railway Executive Committee. This was the Railway Advisory Committee, which included men from a number of the railway companies. The Ministry of Transport Act of 5

August 1919 ushered in a new government department – the Ministry of Transport, with Sir Eric Geddes appointed as Minister of Transport.

The Railway Act of 1921 rejected nationalisation in favour of privately owned regional monopolies. This was put forward by Sir Eric Geddes, who saw this as a way to dispense with unprofitable competition between railway companies.

There is little doubt that the role that the railways played in First World War led to the realisation that they were too valuable to the country to be allowed to continue to operate as they had done before the war. The need for a more unified system was obvious and it perhaps took a war to direct the minds of both the government and the railway owners to move part of the way towards this.

In 1923, the Big Four railway companies were formed by amalgamations. They were the Great Western Railway, the London, Midland and Scottish Railway, the London and North Eastern Railway, and the Southern Railway. The system had escaped nationalisation and it was to take another war to eventually result in permanent government control and the final unification of Britain's railway system.

The Railway Companies after the War

The Big Four

Group 1: Southern Group (Southern Railway)

Constituent companies

London & South Western

London, Brighton & South Coast

South Eastern

London, Chatham & Dover

South Eastern & Chatham

Subsidiary companies

Bridgwater

Brighton & Dyke

Freshwater, Yarmouth & Newport
  (Isle of Wight)

Hayling

Isle of Wight

Isle of Wight Central

Lee-on-the-Solent

London & Greenwich

Mid Kent

North Cornwall

Plymouth & Dartmoor

Plymouth, Devonport & South
  Western Junction

Sidmouth

Victoria Station & Pimlico

Group 2: Western Group (Great Western Railway)

Constituent companies

Great Western

Alexandra (Newport & South
  Wales) Docks & Railways

Barry

Cambrian

Cardiff

Rhymney

Taff Vale

Subsidiary companies

Brecon & Merthyr Tydfil Junction

Burry Port & Gwendraeth Valley

Cleobury Mortimer & Ditton
  Priors Light Railway

Didcot, Newbury & Southampton
Exeter
Ffestiniog
Forest of Dean Central
Gwendraeth Valleys
Lampeter, Aberaeron & New
    Quay Light
Liskeard & Looe
Llanelli & Mynydd Mawr
Mawddwy
Midland & South Western
    Junction
Neath & Brecon
Penarth Extension

Penarth Harbour, Dock &
    Railway
Port Talbot Railway & Docks
Princetown
Rhondda & Swansea Bay
Ross & Monmouth
Shropshire
South Wales Mineral
Teign Valley
Vale of Glamorgan
Van
Welshpool & Llanfair Light
West Somerset
Wrexham & Ellesmere

Group 3: North Western, Midland & West Scottish (London Midland & Scottish Railway)

Constituent companies

London & North Western
Midland
Lancashire & Yorkshire
North Staffordshire

Furness
Caledonian
Glasgow & South Western
Highland

Subsidiary companies

Arbroath & Forfar
Brechin & Edzell District
Callander & Oban
Cathcart District
Charnwood Forest
Cleator & Workington Junction
Cockermouth, Keswick & Penrith
Dearne Valley
Dornoch Light
Dundee & Newtyle
Harborne
Killin

Knott End
Lancashire & Ayrshire
Leek & Manifold Light
Maryport & Carlisle
Mold & Denbigh Junction
North & South Western Junction
North London
Portpatrick & Wigtownshire
    Joint
Shropshire Union Railways &
    Canal
Solway Junction

Stratford-upon-Avon & Midland
  Junction
Tottenham & Forest gate

Wick & Lybster Light
Wirral
Yorkshire Dales

Group 4: North Eastern, Eastern and East Scottish (London & North Eastern)

Constituent companies

North Eastern
Great Central
Great Eastern
Great Northern

Hull & Barnsley
North British
Great North of Scotland

Subsidiary companies

Brackenhill Light
Colne Valley & Halstead
East & West Yorkshire Union
East Lincolnshire
Edinburgh & Bathgate
Forcett
Forth & Clyde Junction
Gifford & Garvald Light
Great North of England, Clarence
  & Hartlepool Junction
Horncastle
Humber Commercial Railway &
  Dock
Kilsyth & Bonnybridge
Lauder Light

London & Blackwall
Mansfield
Mid-Suffolk Light
Newburgh & North Fife
North Lindsey Light
Nottingham & Grantham
  Railway & Canal
Nottingham Joint Station
Nottingham Suburban
Seaforth & Sefton
Sheffield District
South Yorkshire Junction
Stamford & Essendine
West Riding Railway Committee

Companies not included in the big four

Alderney Railway
Ashover Light Railway
Bideford Westward Ho! &
  Appledore Railway
Bishops Castle Railway

Brighton Electric Railway
Camborne and Redruth Tramway
Campbeltown & Machrihanish
  Railway
Central London Railway

City & South London Railway
Corringham Light Railway
Corris Railway
Derwent Valley Light Railway
District Railway
Easingwold Railway
East Kent Railway
Felixstowe Dock Railway
Ffestiniog Railway
Glasgow Subway
Glyn Valley Railway
Guernsey Railway
Hellingly Hospital Railway
Hundred of Manhood & Selsey
   Tramway
Isle of Man Railway
Kent & East Sussex Railway
Jersey Eastern Railway
Jersey Railway & Tramways
Liverpool Overhead Railway
London Electric Railway
Manchester Ship Canal
Manx Electric Railway
Mersey Docks Railway
Mersey Railway
Metropolitan Railway
Milford Haven Dock & Railway

Mumbles Railway
Nidd Valley Railway
North Sunderland Railway
North Wales Narrow Gauge
   Railway
Pentewan Railway
Portmadoc, Beddgelert & South
   Snowdon Railway
Ravenglass and Eskdale Railway
Rowrah and Kelton Fell Railway
Rye & Camber Tramway
Shropshire & Montgomeryshire
   Railway
Snailbeach District Railways
Snowdon Mountain Tramroad
Southwold Railway
Stocksbridge Railway
Swansea Improvements &
   Tramways Company
Talyllyn Railway
Trafford Park Railway
Wantage Tramway
Weston, Clevedon and Portishead
   Railway
Wolverton & Stony Stratford
   Tramway

Appendix II

First World War Railway Memorials in the UK

Note: This may not be an exhaustive list and I would be very interested to hear of any I have missed. I would also like to thank the Railway Heritage Trust for its help in compiling this list.

Aberdeen Station – Great North of Scotland Railway Company

Aintree, Old Roan Station – Merseyside railwaymen

Alrewas, National Memorial Arboretum – London, Brighton & South Coast accounts staff; Lancashire & Yorkshire accounts department; London, Midland & Scottish Railway accounts department; London & North Western Railway audit office

Ashford, Ashford Library – Ashford Railway Works Chief Mechanical Engineers Department roll of honour

Attenborough station – railway station staff

Ayr Station – Glasgow & South Western Railway

Bangor, St David's Church – Bangor Railway Institute Boys Corps

Barrow Central Station – Furness Railway Company

Barry, Dock Office – Barry Railway Company

Belfast Central station – Belfast & County Down Railway Company, and Great Northern Railway

Belfast Translink Railway Workshops – Northern Ireland Railways

Bere Ferrers, St Andrews Church – New Zealand Expeditionary Force railway accident

Birkenhead Station – N. Tunna George Cross

Birmingham New Street station – London & North Western Railway

Birmingham Moor Street station – Great Western Railway

Bishopstoke, St Mary's Church – church bells, one dedicated to railway staff

Brighton station – London, Brighton & South Coast Railway

Bristol Library – Bristol Goods station staff

Bristol Temple Meads station – Great Western Railway roll of honour, and Midland Railway goods dept

Bury station – Lancashire & Yorkshire Carriage and Wagon dept

Cardiff Central station – Cardiff Railway Company

Cardiff, Pierhead Buildings, Bute Docks – Cardiff Railway Company roll of honour

Cardiff Queen Street station – Taff Vale Railway Company roll of honour

Carmarthen station – Great Western Railway local staff

Chester station – Great Western roll of honour, and London & North Western Locomotive Department

Colchester, East Anglian Railway Museum – Great Eastern Railway stores staff, Gidea Park, and Colne Valley & Halstead Railway staff

Coventry station – local soldiers

Crewe Railway Works Garden of Remembrance – Crewe Railway Works; London & North Western Railway; and London, Midland & Scottish Railways

Crewe Weston Road car park – London & North Western Railway office staff

Darlington Station Museum – Robert Stephenson, and WW1

Derby Carriage & Wagon Works – various Midland Railway

Derby station – Midland Railway

Didcot Railway Museum – Great Western Railway

Dingwall station – Sergeant J. Meikle Victoria Cross

Dover Cruise Terminal – South Eastern & Chatham Railway

Dovercourt All Saints Church – Great Eastern Railway, and Captain C.A. Fryatt grave

Dumbarton Central station – Dumbarton & Balloch Joint Railway

Eastleigh Museum – Eastleigh Railway machine shop

Edgeley Railway Club – Midland Railway loco dept

Edinburgh Waverley station – North British Railway Company, and Scottish Branch Red Cross

Exeter St David's station – Great Western Railway roll of honour

Fulbeck St Nicholas Church – Captain H.H. Else, and railway cleaning staff

Garston Dock Manager's Office – Associated British Ports

Garston LMS Institute – London & North Western Railway, and Speke loco shed

Glasgow Ayr station – Glasgow & South Western Railway

Glasgow Central station – Caledonian Railway

Goole Museum – Lancashire & Yorkshire Railway

Gretna Green Blacksmith's shop – Quintinshill railway accident

Guildford station – Guildford station, and Southern Railway

Harwich, Fryatt Hospital – Captain C.A. Fryatt

Heaton Junction admin block – North Eastern Railway roll of honour

Highbridge Gardens of Remembrance – Somerset & Dorset Joint Railway

Holyhead British Legion – SS *Scotia*

Holyhead Museum – London, Midland & Scottish Railway goods and traffic depot

Horwich Locomotive Works – Lancashire & Yorkshire Railway

Huddersfield Town Hall – E. Sykes

Hull Museum – Hull & Barnsley Railway

Hull station – those who passed and fell

Hunstanton, St Edmund's Chapel – Captain C.A. Fryatt, and Mercantile Marine

Inverness station, old railway offices – Highland Railway

Keswick County Square – Cockermouth, Keswick & Penrith Railway

Kettering station – YMCA forces' canteen

Kidderminster station – Great Western Railway, and Birmingham Snow Hill

Kingston upon Hull, Ella Street – Beverley Road signals and telegraph; North Eastern Railway; and Hull Western Docks staff

Lancing, Parish Hall Gardens – Lancing Railway Carriage & Wagon Works

Larbert station – Quintinshill railway accident

Leamington Spa station – Great Western Railway roll of honour

Leconfield, St Martin's Church – Royal Engineers railway troops

Lichfield station – Private W.R. Davies

Leith Rosebank Cemetery Church – 8th Battalion Royal Scots (Quintinshill)

Lincoln Central station – Midland Railway

Liverpool, James Street station – Mersey Railway

Liverpool Lime Street station – railwaymen and women of Liverpool, and Liverpool Pals

Longsight, North West Trains cleaning depot – London & North Western Railway

London, Acton Museum Depot – Underground Electric Railways of London audit staff

London, Baker Street station – Metropolitan Railway

London, East India Dock station – Sergeant Charles Robertson VC

London, Euston station – London & North Western Railway; London, Midland & Scottish Railway; and Lance Corporal J.A. Christie VC

London, Hackney, Hoxton station – North London Railway

London, King's Cross station – Great Northern Railway

London, Paddington station – Great Western Railway

London, Liverpool Street station – Great Eastern Railway, and Captain C.A. Fryatt

London, London Bridge station – London, Brighton & South Coast Railway

London, Marylebone station – Great Central Railway

London, St Pancras station – Midland Railway

London, Victoria station – London Brighton & South Coast Railway; South East & Chatham Railway; and Unknown Warrior plaque.

London, Waterloo station – London & South Western railway arch free buffet for soldiers and sailors

London, Westminster, 55 Broadway – Underground Electric Railway Company of London

London, Westminster Canadian Pacific Railway Office – Canadian Pacific Railway

Manchester, Victoria station – Lancashire & Yorkshire Railway

Manchester, Piccadilly station – Manchester Central Railway staff

Maryport Memorial Gardens – Maryport & Carlisle Railway

Melton Constable, Briston Road – Midland & Great Northern Joint Railway staff

Merthyr Tydfil Library – Great Western Railway roll of honour

Mexborough station – Great Central Railway

Monkwearmouth Station Museum – North Eastern Railway goods depot

Moor Row Working Men's Institute (ex-station) – London & North Western, and Furness Railway

Moseley station – Ernest Sykes VC

Neath station – Lance Corporal A. Lewis VC

Newcastle Heaton Junction – North Eastern Railway roll of honour

Newcastle Co-op Nursery – North Eastern Railway accounts office

Newton Abbot station – Great Western Railway roll of honour

Norchard, Forest of Dean Museum – Great Western Railway roll of honour

Nottingham station – Midland Railway goods station staff

Oswestry, Cambrian Railway Museum – Cambrian Railways roll of honour

Oswestry, Cae Glas Park – Cambrian Railways

Parkeston, Captain Fryatt public house – Captain C.A. Fryatt

Perth station – Perth station staff

Portsea, St Anne's Church – Lieutenant Commander C.H.E. Head (Quintinshill)

Preston station – free buffet WW1, and Preston Pals

Rotherham Steel Terminal – Fallen of WW1

Robertsbridge, Salehurst Church – Private Henry Osborn, and Kent & East Sussex Railway engineer's dept

Rugby station – steam shed roll of honour

Salehurst St Mary Virgin Church – Private H. Osborne, and Kent & East Sussex Railway staff

Shakerstone station – Midland Railway engineers dept Burton section

Sheffield Royal Victoria Holiday Inn – Great Central Railwaymen

Shenfield station – station staff

Shildon North Eastern Railway Institute Museum – North Eastern Railway

Shrewsbury station – London & North Western Railway, and Great Western Railway

Southampton Central Road – Old Contemptibles

Southampton Fremantle Community Academy – Captain C.A. Fryatt

Sowerby Bridge station – Lancashire & Yorkshire Railway

Springburn, North Glasgow College – North British Loco Company

Stoke-on-Trent station – North Staffordshire Railway Company

Stratford-upon-Avon station – Stratford-upon-Avon & Midland Junction Railway

Stockport station – Private W. Wood VC

Swindon, Great Western Railway Museum – various GWR departments

Swindon, Macarthur Glen Shopping Village – Great Western Railway Works

Swinton, St Margaret's Church – Corporal T.N. Jackson VC

Tan-y-Bwlch station – Ffestiniog Railway

Taunton station – Great Western Railway roll of honour

Warrington, DB Shenker Building – London & North Western Railway locomotive dept

Wolverhampton station – London & North Western goods dept

Worcester Railway Museum – Great Western Railway roll of honour

York station – London & North Eastern Railway station foreman W. Milner

York, Rougier Street – London & North Eastern Railway Company

York National Railway Museum – Midland Railway Bristol goods staff, and various other memorials

Glossary

BCDR	Belfast & County Down Railway
BEF	British Expeditionary Force
EKLR	East Kent Light Railway
GCR	Great Central Railway
GER	Great Eastern Railway
GNRI	Great Northern Railway of Ireland
GNR	Great Northern Railway
GWR	Great Western Railway
LB&SCR	London, Brighton & South Coast Railway
L&NWR	London & North Western Railway
L&SWR	London & South Western Railway
LT&SR	London, Tilbury & Southend Railway
L&YR	Lancashire & Yorkshire Railway
NBR	North British Railway
NER	North Eastern Railway
RE	Royal Engineers
ROD	Railway Operating Division
SE&CR	South East & Chatham Railway

Bibliography

Books

Bishop, D. & Davis, K., *Railways and War*, Blandford Press, 1974
Blackwell, E. & Axe, E., *Romford to Beirut*, R.W. Humphries, 1926
Hamilton, J.A.B., *Britain's Railways in WWI*, George Allen & Unwin, 1967
Kidner, R.W., *The Light Railways of Britain*, Oakwood Press, 1947
Junger, E., *Storm of Steel*, Allen Lane, 1961
Pratt, E., *British Railways and the Great War Vol 1*, Selwyn & Blount, 1921
Sassoon, S., *Memoirs of a Foxhunting Man*, Folio, 1979
Sassoon, S., *Memoirs of an Infantry Officer*, Faber & Faber, 1930
Sassoon, S., *Sherston's Progress*, Folio, 1978
Sullivan, Maj W.W., *Accomplishments of the Military Railways*, Railway
  Accounting Officer Association, 1919
Westwood, J., *Railways at War*, Osprey, 1980
Williams, A., *Life in a Railway Factory*, Duckworth & Company, 1915

Periodicals

Great War Magazine: 20 April 1918, 27 April 1918
Great Western Magazine: December 1916
Railway Magazine: May 1915, June 1915, September 1915, February 1916, May
  1916, October 1916, February 1917, December 1931, April 1935, May 1935,
  November 1937, February 1940, March 1940, July 1941, November 1941,
  January & February 1947
The Great Eastern Railway Magazine: May 1914, September 1914, November
  1914
The Great War: I was There: 4 August 1914, 17 August 1914, 4 October 1914,
  12 May 1915
The Railway and Travel Monthly Magazine: February 1917
War Budget Magazine: 5 April 1917
The Times: 5 January 1915, 12 February 1915, 13 February 1915, 2 April 1915,
  25 September 1915, 18 November 1915, 15 March 1916, 4 September 1916,
  12 June 1917, 23 August 1917, 2 May 1918, 14 May 1918

National Archive Documents

MH 47/34/68 Harry Holland
MH 47/75/3 Cyril Baker
MH 47/142/3 Schedule of protected occupations for men

Index